Ending
Your Day
Right

Ending Your Day Right

DEVOTIONS FOR
EVERY EVENING OF THE YEAR

Joyce Meyer

Faith
Words

NEW YORK BOSTON NASHVILLE

Let my prayer be set
before You as incense, the
lifting up of my hands as
the evening sacrifice.

PSALM 141:2 NKJV

Introduction

God wants you to enjoy everyday life—it is His will for you. As a Christian you can have a quality of life that far exceeds your expectations, but it requires cooperation on your part. Jesus said in John 15:10-11 that if you obey His instructions and abide in His love, your joy and gladness will be full, complete, and overflowing.

Enjoying life to the fullest begins by making a decision to set aside time each day to pray and meditate on God's Word and to learn His will and direction for your life. The people who most enjoy life are those who spend time with God, seeking His direction and then following His leading.

Starting your day right by spending time with God in the morning is an important part of enjoying life. But spending time with God at night before you go to bed is an extra special time—an unhurried time that allows you to relax in the presence of God and reflect on the activities of the day.

It is a great time to acknowledge and thank Him

for His presence with you throughout the day, and to seek His help with any unresolved problems or concerns you may have. Consider His invitation in Matthew 11:28-29:

> Come to Me, all you who labor and are heavy-laden and overburdened, and I will cause you to rest. [I will ease and relieve and refresh your souls.] Take My yoke upon you and learn of Me, for I am gentle (meek) and humble (lowly) in heart, and you will find rest (relief and ease and refreshment and recreation and blessed quiet) for your souls.

My purpose in writing this book is to help you focus on God at the end of your busy days. In the quiet solitude of the night He will refresh and re-store you, lead you in paths of righteousness (see Psalm 23:3), and teach you how to enjoy every day of your life.

> It is vain for you to rise up early, to take rest late, to eat the bread of (anxious) toil—for He gives (blessings) to His beloved in sleep. PSALM 127:2

Ending
Your Day
Right

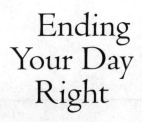

You Can Have a New Beginning

Do not [earnestly] remember the former things;
neither consider the things of old. Behold, I am doing
a new thing!

ISAIAH 43:18-19

God created us to need new beginnings—places where we can release our faith and say, "This is a place of new beginnings for me, a place to have a fresh start." The dawn of a new year is always a good time for a fresh start.

You can experience the abundant life Jesus says you can have, but it requires making a decision to let go of the past. Unless you refuse to go on the way you have been, no change will come. God wants to change things for you, but He is waiting for your total cooperation.

Seldom do your circumstances change without something first changing in you. So if you want to experience God's "new thing" this year, release your faith right now and say, "This is a place of new beginnings for me." Then watch for the results.

Seek to Know God Better

[For my determined purpose is] that I may know Him [that I may progressively become more deeply and intimately acquainted with Him, perceiving and recognizing and understanding the wonders of His Person more strongly and more clearly].

PHILIPPIANS 3:10

This was the cry of the apostle Paul's heart as he sought to have such a deep relationship with Christ that the trials of life would barely be noticeable.

At the beginning of this new year, it is a wise thing for you to seek also. There are plenty of problems in life that can weigh you down and cause you to become discouraged, but God wants to provide the strength and power you need to be victorious in every battle of life. Such a relationship requires that you seek God like never before.

So start this year right by becoming more deeply and intimately acquainted with the One who has all power in heaven and earth.

Trust in the Power of Hope

Hope deferred makes the heart sick, but when the
desire is fulfilled, it is a tree of life.

PROVERBS 13:12

I define *hope* as "the happy anticipation of good things." You can hope for something good to happen to you by learning how to celebrate and enjoy life.

Everything in life is a process in motion. Without movement and progression there is no life. As long as you live you are always heading somewhere, and you should enjoy yourself on the way. God created you to be a goal-oriented visionary. Without a vision you become bored and hopeless.

But there's something about hope that makes people lighthearted and happy. Hope is a powerful spiritual force that is activated through your positive attitude. God is positive and He wants positive things to happen to you, but that probably won't happen unless you have hope and faith.

Expect God to bring good out of every circumstance in your life. Whatever happens, trust in the Lord . . . and trust in the power of hope!

Watch Your Words

There are those who speak rashly, like the piercing
of a sword, but the tongue of the wise brings healing.

PROVERBS 12:18

Your life is greatly impacted by the words that have been spoken to you. Likewise, your words impact the lives of those around you— for better or for worse. That's a sobering thought.

Many people have been crippled with insecurity because their parents spoke words of judgment, criticism, and failure to them. These wounded people can be healed by receiving God's unconditional love, but it takes time to overcome the wrong image they have of themselves.

That's why it is important to use your words for blessing, healing, and building up instead of for cursing, wounding, and tearing down.

If you've been wounded by words, be quick to receive God's unconditional love. Let Him heal any unhealthy images you may have of yourself. If you have been fortunate enough to escape such damage, determine that your words will bring blessing and healing to others.

Possess Your Soul

By your steadfastness and patient endurance you
shall win the true life of your souls.

LUKE 21:19

You need to learn not to let your mind and emotions get the best of you, especially when it involves things over which you have no control.

Suppose you are on your way to an important interview and get caught in a traffic jam. How do you react? Is it worth getting all upset and unleashing a wild spirit? Wouldn't it be much better for you and everyone else if you just remained calm, even if you were late for the interview? If you have done your best God will do the rest.

Refuse to get upset when things don't go as you planned. Refuse to allow your mind, will, and emotions to rule your spirit. In your patience you will learn to possess your soul.

Praise Your Way to Victory

Be not afraid or dismayed . . .
for the battle is not yours, but God's.

2 CHRONICLES 20:15

If life sometimes seems to be a battle that causes you to feel upset and fearful, you'll be glad to know you were not meant to fight the battle alone. The Bible says the battle is God's.

God never loses a battle. And when you work with Him according to His plan, you won't either.

During trying times, do you worry or worship? Praise and worship should not be limited to a few minutes in church. If you're not worshipping at home on a regular basis you may feel like the victim instead of the victor.

But God's Word clearly details the Holy Ghost-anointed battle plan to combat every challenge you face. When you begin to substitute praise for petition and worship for worry, God will move on your behalf.

Choose Inner Purity

The inward adorning and beauty of the hidden
person of the heart, with the incorruptible and
unfading charm of a gentle and peaceful
spirit . . . is very precious in the sight of God.

I PETER 3:4

In light of this Scripture, how would you classify your thoughts, attitudes, imaginations, opinions, and judgments? Are they clean or corrupt? Pure or carnal?

Inner purity is a challenge that requires you to watch over your inner life with determination and diligence. In the beginning you may feel that most of your thoughts, imaginations, and attitudes are corrupt. But as you persist, new habits develop, and with regular maintenance you can enjoy inner purity.

What you do outwardly—the things that people see—determines your reputation with man. But your inner life determines your reputation with God.

Choosing inner purity is something you do unto the Lord to honor Him. No wonder He says a pure heart is precious in His sight!

Choose God's Secret Place

He who dwells in the secret place of the Most
High shall remain stable and fixed under the shadow
of the Almighty [Whose power no foe can withstand].
I will say of the Lord, He is my Refuge and my
Fortress, my God; on Him I lean and rely, and in Him
I [confidently] trust!

PSALM 91:1-2

This Scripture holds the key to overcoming worry, anxiety, discouragement, disappointment, depression, despair, and disease. It is simply trusting God.

Perhaps you want to trust God, but it seems you just don't know how. Trusting God requires knowing Him—knowing His character and having experience with Him. Going through trials with God by your side builds your faith.

So when you face problems, you can choose trust or torment. Choose to trust God and dwell in the "secret place," enjoying divine provision in the midst of attacks and walking through dark times in His presence.

Receive God's Healing and Restoration

The Spirit of the Lord God is upon me . . . to bind up and heal the brokenhearted, to proclaim liberty to the [physical and spiritual] captives and the opening of the prison and of the eyes to those who are bound.

ISAIAH 61:1

If you are struggling with emotional distress or a broken heart, God wants to renew your mind, restore your soul, and give you a fresh start.

I don't know your circumstances, past or present, but you may have hurts that are holding you back and keeping you captive.

I know firsthand how that feels. But I also know what it's like to be healed and restored. As I received the truth of God's Word and began to understand that I didn't have to stay trapped in my past, I experienced emotional healing and deliverance from bondage.

God loves you unconditionally and He wants to do the same for you. So learn how to receive from God . . . and be made whole.

Accept God's Grace

[God] . . . is able to do immeasurably more than all we ask or imagine, according to his power that is at work within us.

EPHESIANS 3:20 NIV

Life is hectic—and if you try to do everything yourself you'll stay exhausted. Rushing and struggling to keep up the pace wears you out physically, mentally, emotionally, and spiritually. But you can make some changes.

First, examine all your activities and allow the Holy Spirit to show you the things that drain your energy and don't produce worthwhile fruit. Then be willing to give them up. You may even have to choose between the good and the best.

Second, learn to receive more of God's grace. Grace is power—God getting involved and doing through you what you could never do on your own. His power can help you accomplish more than you could imagine. So accept His help and start enjoying life.

Take Authority over the Devil

Be well balanced, . . . vigilant and cautious at all times; for that enemy of yours, the devil, roams around like a lion roaring [in fierce hunger], seeking someone to seize upon and devour.

1 PETER 5:8

Satan's attacks are fierce in these last days but you don't need to run from his roar. As a child of God you have the authority to defeat him in the name of Jesus.

Satan can attack your mind, will, and emotions. He will attack your body with weariness and all manner of illness. His lies are endless and persistent and he delights in playing on your emotions. But you can learn to discern and aggressively confront every satanic assault, and be victorious over his evil plans.

Exercising authority over the enemy is more than verbal commands . . . your words and actions must go together. Speaking or praying the Word releases faith, but you must also walk in new levels of obedience. So follow God's plan and put the devil on the run.

Let God Restore Your Soul

The Lord is my Shepherd . . . He refreshes and
restores my life . . . He leads me in the paths of
righteousness . . . not for my earning it . . .
but for His name's sake.

PSALM 23:1,3

This psalm is a great comfort and encouragement. Your Shepherd refreshes and restores your life, or as the King James Version says, your soul.

The word *restore* means, "to return to a former condition," to refresh. In this psalm David is telling you God will return you to the state you were in before you erred from following the good plan He had predestined for you before your birth.

God's plan for you is not failure, misery, poverty, sickness, or disease. His plan is for you to have a wonderful life full of health, happiness, and fulfillment.

So don't let the devil steal it away from you. The evening is a great time to quietly wait in the presence of the Lord and allow Him to refresh and restore your soul.

Be Confident in Christ

I have strength for all things in Christ
Who empowers me [I am ready for anything
and equal to anything through Him Who infuses
inner strength into me].

PHILIPPIANS 4:13

You were created by a great God to do great things. But without confidence you will never fulfill your destiny. It is important, however, to remember you are to be confident not in yourself but in Christ who dwells in you.

Satan tries to steal your confidence, but you must resist him at all times. If he has tormented you with fears about your worth and abilities, boldly remind him God is with you and you are equal to anything.

It is encouraging to know God is able even when you are not. He has His eye on you and is waiting for you to show confidence in Him. Faith opens the door for God's greatness to be seen through your life, so trust Him and enjoy the peace and power of a confident life.

Dwell in Peace

Depart from evil and do good; seek, inquire for,
and crave peace and pursue (go after) it!

PSALM 34:14

In our strife-torn world, do you ever long for a few peaceful moments? That is what God wants for you. He instructs you in His Word to live in unity and harmony and to pursue peace.

Why then is it so difficult to get through a day without being invaded by the spirit of strife? Satan works through the weaknesses in your flesh to keep the atmosphere in your life and the attitudes of your heart in continual turmoil. He seeks to draw you away from peace and into strife, which brings devastation and destruction.

But God's power is greater than the devil's, and when you come against strife in the name of Jesus you render it powerless to rob you of the peace and joy that is your divine inheritance. Take a few moments in the quiet of this evening to enjoy the wonderful peace and presence of God, and you will enjoy a good night's sleep.

Let God Be Good to You

The Lord [earnestly] waits [expecting, looking, and longing] to be gracious to you; and therefore He lifts Himself up, that He may have mercy on you and show loving-kindness to you.

ISAIAH 30:18

Isn't this a wonderful verse? It tells you God is waiting to be good to you. He's actually looking and longing for an opportunity to show His goodness. He is a God of justice and He desires to make every wrong thing right. But He can only be good to those who are waiting for Him to be good to them—those who believe His promises.

Are you available? Don't fall into Satan's trap of being negative. Don't believe it when he tells you your past is really not past and your future is bleak. Choose to believe God and get ready to receive the wonderful gifts He is waiting to give to you. Go to sleep meditating on this thought: *Something good is going to happen to me!*

Don't Give Up!

Let us not be weary in well doing: for in due
season we shall reap, if we faint not.

GALATIANS 6:9 KJV

Do you ever feel like giving up? Perhaps you're discouraged about your finances or you're facing problems with your health, your marriage, or your children. Sometimes problems seem so overwhelming that the road ahead seems too steep to climb.

We all go through these times. I've wanted to give up and quit many times through the years. But when I realized I had nothing interesting to go back to, I determined to keep pressing on.

Even though continuing to move forward is sometimes painful, it is far better than giving up and sliding backwards. God is doing a good work in you so He can do more for you and through you. So ask Him to fill you with holy determination tonight and keep moving in the right direction.

Learn to Love

I give you a new commandment: that you should
love one another. Just as I have loved you, so you too
should love one another.

JOHN 13:34

How much do you know about real love . . . God's kind of love?

Everybody knows love is always spoken of in connection with Christianity. There are lots of sermons on love—it's a pretty plain and simple subject. Everybody talks about love.

But where are all the people who love?

God's kind of love is unconditional and always available. He extends His love toward you and He wants you to receive it and be blessed. Then He wants you to give it away to others.

What the world needs now is love—real love. I have discovered that lonely and hurting people often don't expect you to meet their needs . . . they simply want to be loved and understood.

If you're in need of real love, receive it from God right now. Then let it flow through you to bless others.

God Has Not Forgotten You

God is faithful; he will not let you be tempted
beyond what you can bear. But when you are
tempted, he will also provide a way out so that you
can stand up under it.

1 CORINTHIANS 10:13 NIV

The world is full of people struggling with trials and temptations and looking for a way out. If you have ever felt pressed on every side and couldn't find an escape, or confused and didn't know what to do, you know what a desperate and lonely feeling that can be.

The Word tells you God is faithful and He will provide a way for you, but He doesn't always show us the way immediately. That is when you must wait . . . and trust.

Waiting on God purifies your faith and builds character in you. You may not like waiting, but God's way is perfect! So be assured God has not forgotten you. Trust Him, and in His time He will reveal His perfect plan for you. While you're waiting, don't forget to enjoy your life.

Expect the Blessings of God

Wait and hope for and expect the Lord; be brave
and of good courage and let your heart be
stout and enduring.

PSALM 27:14

Sometimes you may feel discouraged, miserable, and depressed. In those times you need to take a close look at what's been going on in your mind. Isaiah 26:3 tells you when you keep your mind on the Lord you will have "perfect and constant peace."

By focusing on the goodness of God and waiting, hoping, and expecting Him to encourage you and fill you with His peace and joy, you can overcome negative thoughts that drag you down.

Think and speak positively. Begin believing right now that you are about to see God's goodness in your life. Wait, hope, and expect His blessings to be abundant in your life.

Say Yes to God

No one's ever seen or heard anything like this,
Never so much as imagined anything quite like it—
what God has arranged for those who love him.

1 CORINTHIANS 2:9 THE MESSAGE

God prearranged and paid for you to have and enjoy a good life before you ever showed up on planet Earth. Then He sent the Holy Spirit to guide you into all truth and the blessings He wants you to have. The key to receiving is simply obedience.

When you don't obey God's promptings you get off track and fail to enjoy all the good things He has in mind for you. Don't let the devil trick you into losing out on God's superabundance because of disobedience.

Begin sowing seeds of prompt obedience and divine blessing will overtake you. Radical, outrageous obedience will bring radical, outrageous blessings. Obeying God during the day helps us sleep good at night.

Overcome Fear with Faith

*God has not given us a spirit of fear, but of power
and of love and of a sound mind.*

2 TIMOTHY 1:7 NKJV

Have you ever thought how great it would be if you could live without ever having to deal with fear?

Of course, there are healthy fears that alert you to danger in time to avoid it—and these are good because they protect you. But there are many other fears Satan tries to put on you that should not be legitimate concerns. They are **F**alse **E**vidence **A**ppearing **R**eal, and they are intended to keep you from having the power, love, and sound mind God wants you to have.

Fear is a spirit that must be confronted head on—it will not just go away. But God has given you the power to boldly confront your fear and break its hold on your life.

So when fear knocks on your door, send faith to answer!

Let God Be God

For who has known or understood the mind (the counsels and purposes) of the Lord so as to guide and instruct Him and give Him knowledge?

1 CORINTHIANS 2:16

It is not your job to give God guidance, counsel, or direction. It is your job to listen to God and let Him tell you what is going on and what you are to do about it—leaving the rest to Him to work out according to His knowledge and will, not yours.

God is God—and you are not. You need to recognize that truth and simply trust yourself to Him, because He is greater than you are in every way. You are created in His image, but He is still above and beyond you. His thoughts and ways are higher than yours. So listen to God tonight, be obedient to Him, and He will teach you His ways. Cast off your care, releasing the weight of all your burdens and sleep peacefully.

Allow God to Change You

*And while He was in Bethany . . . a woman came
with an alabaster jar of ointment (perfume) of pure
nard, very costly and precious; and she broke the jar
and poured [the perfume] over His head.*

MARK 14:3

So often people are afraid of brokenness.
But if your outer man is broken, the powerful things inside you can pour forth. The perfume
of the Holy Spirit is within you, but the alabaster
box, which represents the flesh, has to be broken for
that sweet fragrance to be released. The flesh is naturally prideful and stubborn.

To fully release the power of the Holy Spirit
within you, you must allow God to do with you as
He wills, knowing that everything in life changes.

If you are to have stability in your life you must
remember life is a continual process in which everything—including you—is constantly changing. You
must hope in God, the only one who "is the same
yesterday, today, and forever" (Hebrews 13:8 NKJV).

Stay in Balance

I have learned how to be content (satisfied to the point where I am not disturbed or disquieted) in whatever state I am.

PHILIPPIANS 4:11

Stability is maturity. To grow up in God is to come to the place where you can be content no matter what your situation or circumstances may be because you are rooted and grounded, not in things, but in the Lord.

Paul was emotionally and spiritually mature because he knew whatever state he was in would pass. He had learned the secret of facing every situation of life, whether good or bad.

God wants to bless you and use you as a vessel through which His Holy Spirit can work. But in order for that to happen you must learn how to handle both the good times and the bad. That's why it is so important to remember that whatever comes your way, "This too shall pass." The good times and the bad never last forever, but *through Christ* we can handle either with joy and stability.

You're Just Passing Through

Yes, though I walk through the [deep, sunless]
valley of the shadow of death, I will fear or dread no
evil, for You are with me; Your rod [to protect] and
Your staff [to guide], they comfort me.

PSALM 2 3:4

The psalmist David said he walked through the valley of the shadow of death. That's what you must do in all the situations and circumstances of this life. You must remember you are just passing through.

When you feel as if you're stuck in a situation that will never change, you must allow God to guide you through it. When the devil says, "You're trapped," boldly say to him, "Wrong! I'm just passing through!"

Shadrach, Meshach, and Abednego were cast into the fiery furnace, but God brought them safely through the fire (see Daniel 3).

God's Word says He will provide that same protection and deliverance to all who put their faith and trust in Him. So believe it as you walk through the valley of your own situation.

We Shall All Be Changed!

We shall not all fall asleep [in death], but we
shall all be changed (transformed) in a moment, in
the twinkling of an eye, at the [sound of the]
last trumpet call.

1 CORINTHIANS 15:51-52

We all like "suddenlies," and God promises that whatever remains to be accomplished in us will be done "suddenly" when Jesus returns to the earth. Until then, we can confidently trust He is working in us through His word and Spirit on a regular basis. If you are spending time in God's word and believing He is doing work in you, then you are changing from one degree of glory to another.

You don't have to be discouraged about your spiritual growth or in your walk with God, because no matter what remains to be done in the transformation of your old man into your new man, it will be finished at the appearing of Jesus in the heavenlies.

If the devil tries to tell you you're going to stay the way you are forever, he is lying. God promises in His word that He has begun a good work in you and He also will finish it (see Philippians 1:6).

Retire from Self-Care

*Believe in the Lord Jesus Christ [give yourself
up to Him, take yourself out of your own keeping
and entrust yourself into His keeping] and you
will be saved.*

ACTS 16:31

God wants to take care of you, and He can do a much better job of it if you will avoid a problem called *independence*, which is really self-care.

The desire to take care of yourself is based on fear. You are afraid of what might happen if you entrust yourself totally to God and He doesn't come through for you. The root problem of independence is you trust yourself more than you trust God.

People love to have a back-up plan. You may ask God to get involved in your life, but if He doesn't respond as quickly as you'd like, you take control back into your own hands.

But God has a plan for you—and His plan is much better than yours. So give yourself to Him and see what happens. I promise you won't be disappointed.

Stand Strong Against the Adversary

For a wide door of opportunity for effectual
[service] has opened to me [there, a great and
promising one], and [there are] many adversaries.

1 CORINTHIANS 16:9

It is true that whenever you do anything for God, the adversary will oppose you. But you must remember that greater is He who is in you than he who is in the world (see 1 John 4:4).

You should not have to spend your life struggling against the devil in order to serve God. Instead of wearing yourself out trying to fight spiritual enemies, you should learn to stand strong in the authority given to you by Jesus.

The best way to overcome the devil and his demons is simply to stay in God's will by obeying His Word and God will work things out according to His divine plan and purpose.

Depend on the Spirit

*It is the Spirit Who gives life [He is the
Life-giver]; the flesh conveys no benefit whatever.*

JOHN 6:63

If you are to fulfill God's will for you in
this life, the flesh—the selfish, rebellious
sin nature—must die. It must lose its power.

Often you are not fully aware of sinful thoughts,
actions, and attitudes in your heart because you are
so caught up in the outer life. These things must be
faced and dealt with if you are to enjoy the good life
God has planned for you.

Paul said he wanted to do good things, but found
himself always doing wrong things. He described
how miserable this made him. He wanted to be free,
and after much struggling realized that only God
could set him free and that through Jesus Christ He
would. (see Romans 7:18-25).

As you face seasons of testing you must learn
that your flesh benefits you nothing. Only then can
you deny the flesh and depend on the Life-giver to
build His character in you.

Let Go and Let God

Abstain from evil . . . whatever kind it may be.
And may the God of peace Himself sanctify you
through and through . . . and may your spirit
and soul and body be preserved sound and
complete . . . Faithful is He Who is calling
you . . . and utterly trustworthy.

1 THESSALONIANS 5:22-24

These are God's instructions to you for finding peace and joy: Stay away from wrong behavior and allow the Lord of peace to sanctify you, preserve you, complete you, hallow you, and keep you.

These verses are your call from God to a certain kind of holy living. They are also your assurance that it is not you who brings about this holy life but God Himself, who can be trusted utterly to do the work in you and for you.

What then is your part? What is the work that you are to do? What does God require of you? Your part is to believe and to trust the Lord. So let go and let God!

Choose to Please God

Now am I trying to win the favor of men, or of God? Do I seek to please men? If I were still seeking popularity with men, I should not be a bond servant of Christ (the Messiah).

GALATIANS 1:10

The apostle Paul said that in his ministry he had to choose between pleasing men and pleasing God. That is a choice you also must make.

If your goal is to build a name for yourself and win favor with people, it will cause you to live in fear of man rather than in fear of God.

For years I tried to build my own reputation among believers by striving to win the favor of men. But through bitter experience I learned I was submitting to a sort of slavery to people. God helped me realize I could only be truly free in Him.

If you are trying to build your reputation with people, it's time to give up all your own human efforts and simply trust God. He will give you supernatural favor with the people that are right for you.

Gifts of Grace

For by the grace (unmerited favor of God) given to
me I warn everyone among you not to estimate and
think of himself more highly than he ought [not to
have an exaggerated opinion of his own importance],
but to rate his ability with sober judgment, each accord-
ing to the degree of faith apportioned by God to him.

ROMANS 12:3

Proud people compare themselves to others and feel superior if they are able to do something others cannot do. In 1 Corinthians 15:10, the apostle Paul wrote, "But by the grace (the unmerited favor and blessing) of God I am what I am." If you do not realize you are what you are by the grace of God, you will think more highly of yourself than you should.

You should judge yourself soberly, knowing that without God you can do nothing of value. Success only comes by His grace. Your accomplishments and abilities are not yours to take credit for—they are gifts from a loving Father.

The I Am

And God said to Moses, I AM WHO I AM and
WHAT I AM, and I WILL BE WHAT I WILL BE; and
He said, You shall say this to the Israelites: I AM has
sent me to you!

EXODUS 3:14

This awesome scripture holds much more than you may realize at first glance. God is so great there is no way for us to describe Him properly. What was God really saying when He referred to Himself as I AM?

Moses asked a question about God's identity, and evidently the Lord did not want to get into a long dissertation about who He was. It was as if God was saying, "You don't have to worry about Pharaoh or anybody else, I AM able to take care of anything you encounter. Whatever you need, I AM it. Either I have it or I can get it. If it doesn't exist, I will create it. I have everything covered, not only now but for all time. Relax!"

God Approves of You!

*Before I formed you in the womb I knew [and]
approved of you [as My chosen instrument].*

JEREMIAH 1:5

Nobody knows you as well as God does. Yet even though He knows everything about you, including all of your faults, He still approves of you and accepts you. God sees your heart, not just the exterior shell (the flesh) that seems to get you into so much trouble. He does not approve of your wrong behavior, but He is committed to you as an individual. God can hate what you do and yet love you. He has no trouble keeping the two separated.

God never intended for you to feel bad about yourself. He wants you to know yourself well and yet accept yourself. You must be able to say, "I can love what God can love. I don't love everything I do, but I accept myself because God accepts me." God is changing you daily. Ask Him to help you accept and love yourself in spite of your imperfections.

Not In Vain

You shall not use or repeat the name of the Lord
your God in vain [that is, lightly or frivolously, in
false affirmations or profanely]; for the Lord will not
hold him guiltless who takes His name in vain.

EXODUS 20:7

Malachi 1:14 says, "For I am a great King, says the Lord of hosts, and My name is terrible and to be [reverently] feared among the nations." As a Christian, you need to have such reverence for the Lord that you are afraid to speak any of His holy names without purpose. But we often say things like, "Oh God," "My God," and "Dear God" as casual terms of expression.

According to the Bible, we have been given authority to cast out demons, pray for the sick, and preach the gospel in the name of Jesus. How can we expect to see God's power manifested if we use His name seriously one time and frivolously another? If we mix positives with negatives, we will operate with zero power.

A Victorious Church

*And the Lord shall make you the head, and not
the tail; and you shall be above only, and you shall
not be beneath, if you heed the commandments of the
Lord your God.*

DEUTERONOMY 28:13

Surely we are living in the last days, and
the Bible teaches that Satan's attacks will
intensify during these perilous times. The enemy is
a master of deception. He lies, cheats, and steals. Satan launches personal attacks on your marriage, your
children, your job, and your personal property. He
also targets your mind, your emotions, and your physical body.

How do you defend yourself? Ephesians 3:10 says,
"Through the church the complicated, many-sided
wisdom of God . . . might now be made known to
the angelic rulers and authorities (principalities and
powers) in the heavenly sphere." God intends to work
through the church to defeat the enemy. He will do it
through us! He will grant us wisdom in what action to
take and strength to take it. The greater One lives in
us as believers; therefore we have power over Satan.

Thoughts of the Heart

*Either make the tree sound (healthy and good),
and its fruit sound (healthy and good), or make the
tree rotten (diseased and bad), and its fruit rotten
(diseased and bad); for the tree is known and
recognized and judged by its fruit.*

MATTHEW 12:33

The Bible says a tree is known by its fruit, and the same is true of you. You can look at a person's attitude and know what kind of thinking is prevalent in his life. A sweet, kind person does not have mean, vindictive thoughts. By the same token, a truly evil person does not have good, loving thoughts.

Your thoughts bear fruit. Think good thoughts and the fruit in your life will be good. Think bad thoughts and the fruit in your life will be bad. Remember Proverbs 23:7 and allow it to have an impact on your life: for as you think in your heart, so are you.

The Paraclete

But when He, the Spirit of Truth (the Truth-giving Spirit) comes, He will guide you into all the Truth (the whole, full Truth). For He will not speak His own message [on His own authority]; but He will tell whatever He hears [from the Father; He will give the message that has been given to Him], and He will announce and declare to you the things that are to come [that will happen in the future].

JOHN 16:13

God knew you would need help in understanding His plan for you, so He sent the Holy Spirit to dwell inside you. He is your Guide, your Teacher of truth, your Comfort, and your Helper. He is also the Parakletos (Paraclete), which means counselor, advocate, and intercessor.

Jesus was confined to a body and could be only one place at a time. But He knew the Holy Spirit would be with you everywhere you go, all the time, leading and guiding you. Trust the Holy Spirit in you, resting in the knowledge that in Him you are becoming everything God planned for you to be.

Choose Life

*I call heaven and earth to witness this day against
you that I have set before you life and death, the
blessings and the curses; therefore choose life, that you
and your descendants may live.*

DEUTERONOMY 30:19

In this Scripture *life* means, "fresh, strong, lively, and merry." In John 10:10, Jesus said He came that you might have life. According to *Vine's Expository Dictionary of Biblical Words*, in this verse *life* is translated as, "life as God has it, that which the Father has in Himself, and which He gave to the Incarnate Son to have in Himself . . . and which the Son manifested in the world."

Life is not simply a span of time. It is a quality of existence—life as God has it. His life is not filled with fear, stress, worry, or depression. God takes time to enjoy His creation. Adam lost that kind of life due to sin, but you can have it back through Christ Jesus. Choose God's kind of life.

The Real Thing

*You are the salt of the earth, but if salt has lost
its taste (its strength, its quality), how can its saltness
be restored? . . . You are the light of the world. A city
set on a hill cannot be hidden.*

MATTHEW 5:13-14

When people learn you're a Christian,
they want to know if you are "for real."
Many people have tried "religion" and had a bad experience. God uses us to reach the world. If you are
to be effective salt, you must allow Jesus to shine
through your life.

You probably know someone who just lights up
a room. In the same way, Christians who let the light
of Jesus shine can change the whole atmosphere
around them. Unbelievers ought to feel as though
the power has suddenly come on—even if they don't
understand why. When you arrive at your job in the
morning, be salt and light so those around you know
that your relationship with Jesus is the real thing.

A Balancing Act

I came that they may have and enjoy life, and
have it in abundance (to the full, till it overflows).

JOHN 10:10

For years I felt that everything in my life should be work, work, work. As long as I was accomplishing something, as long as I was doing what everyone expected of me, I believed I was pleasing God. Unfortunately I wasn't enjoying my life!

I'll never forget the day my kids wanted me to watch a movie with them. They kept saying, "Mom, come on! You don't have to work all day and either read the Bible or pray the rest of the time. We know you love God. Let's have some fun." I finally decided to watch a movie with them but found myself feeling guilty for doing so.

God had to teach me that there is nothing wrong with spending time with family, taking a day off, or having fun. You can work yourself to death and miss some of God's greatest blessings. Allow Him to bring balance to your life.

Mumbles and Murmurs

*These are inveterate murmurers (grumblers) who
complain [of their lot in life], going after their own
desires [controlled by their passions].*

JUDE 1:16

Sometimes it seems the whole world is complaining. There is so much grumbling and murmuring and so little gratitude and appreciation. People complain about their job and their boss when they should be thankful to have regular work and appreciate the fact they are not living in a shelter for the homeless or standing in a soup line. Many people would be thrilled to have that job, despite its imperfections. They would be more than willing to put up with a not-so-perfect boss in order to have a regular income, live in their own home, and cook their own food.

Maybe you need a better paying job or perhaps you have a boss who treats you unfairly. That is unfortunate, but the way out is not through complaining. Give God thanks tonight for every blessing He has given you.

Standing in Big Shoes

No man shall be able to stand before you all the days of your life. As I was with Moses, so I will be with you; I will not fail you or forsake you.

JOSHUA 1:5

Imagine how Joshua must have felt when God told him he was to take Moses' place and lead the Israelites into the promised land. Moses was an amazing leader. Who would want to try to fill his shoes?

God told Joshua he would succeed not because of anything he had in the natural but because He was with him. Moses was successful only because God was with him. God told Joshua the same thing would hold true for him if he believed. God kept encouraging Joshua to be strong and confident, to take courage and not be afraid. In other words, He told him to believe!

Put your faith and trust in God. He will give you the strength to stand and accomplish whatever He asks you to do.

Blessed Assurance

For I am persuaded beyond doubt (am sure) that
neither death nor life, nor angels nor principalities,
nor things impending and threatening nor things to
come, nor powers, nor height nor depth, nor anything
else in all creation will be able to separate us from the
love of God which is in Christ Jesus our Lord.

ROMANS 8:38-39

You cannot trust unless you believe you are loved. To grow in God and be changed you must trust Him. Often He will lead you in ways you cannot understand. During those times you must have a tight grip on His love for you. The apostle Paul was convinced that nothing would ever be able to separate him from the love of God in Christ Jesus. You need to have that same absolute assurance of God's undying love for you.

Accept God's love for you and make that love the basis for your love for others. Receive His affirmation, knowing that you are changing and becoming all He desires you to be.

A Perfect Love

*And we know (understand, recognize, are conscious
of, by observation and by experience) and believe
(adhere to and put faith in and rely on) the love God
cherishes for us. God is love, and he who dwells and
continues in love dwells and continues in God, and
God dwells and continues in him.*

1 JOHN 4:16

Most people can believe God loves them if they think they deserve it. Problems arise when you feel you do not deserve God's love and yet desperately need it. God's love for you is perfect—and unconditional. When you fail He keeps loving you because His love is not based on you but on Him.

Sin separated you from God, but He loved you so much He sent His only Son, Jesus, to die for you so He could lavish His great love upon you. If you can believe that God, who is so perfect, loves you, then you can believe you are worth loving! When that happens you can accept yourself in a new way that will be life changing. You're special; you have worth and value . . . believe it, receive it, and be all you can be in Christ.

The Narrow Path

*Enter by the narrow gate; for wide is the gate and
broad is the way that leads to destruction, and there
are many who go in by it. Because narrow is the gate
and difficult is the way which leads to life,
and there are few who find it.*

MATTHEW 7:13-14 NKJV

Life as a Christian can sometimes feel like a pressure cooker. God speaks to us about issues and works to bring correction. There are things in our lives that hinder us from being all God wants us to be and He deals with them because He loves us and wants to release His best into our lives.

This is an ongoing process. God shows us something, we usually wrestle with Him for awhile, and then we finally change. He lets us rest awhile and then shows us something new that needs to be dealt with.

We once walked on a wide and reckless road that led to destruction, but now we are guided down a narrow path that leads to life. There is no room on the narrow path for our old fleshly, selfish ways. No wonder Paul said, "It is no longer I who live, but Christ . . . lives in me" (Galatians 2:20).

Shake It Off!

*Now Paul had gathered a bundle of sticks, and he
was laying them on the fire when a viper crawled out
because of the heat and fastened itself on his hand.
When the natives saw the little animal hanging from
his hand, they said to one another, Doubtless this
man is a murderer, for though he has been saved from
the sea, Justice [the goddess of avenging] has not
permitted that he should live. Then [Paul simply]
shook off the small creature into the fire and
suffered no evil effects.*

ACTS 28:3-5

When Paul was shipwrecked on the island
of Malta, a deadly snake that was driven
out by the heat of the fire bit him. He simply shook
the creature off into the flames. You should follow
Paul's example and do the same in your own life.

Whatever may be troubling you, shake it off!
God has great things planned for you. The dreams of
the future leave no room for the snakebites of the
past.

A Heart of Flesh

I will give them one heart [a new heart] and I
will put a new spirit within them; and I will take the
stony [unnaturally hardened] heart out of their flesh,
and will give them a heart of flesh [sensitive and
responsive to the touch of their God].

EZEKIEL 11:19

God puts a sense of right and wrong deep within your conscience, but if you rebel too many times, you can become hard-hearted. If that happens, you need to let Him soften your heart so you can be sensitive to the leadership of the Holy Spirit.

The only way to develop a heart of flesh is to spend time with God. You must be in His presence on a regular basis to hear what He is saying. God often speaks gently, and those who are busy doing their own thing will not hear His still, small voice. Tonight as you spend time in the Lord's presence, ask Him to soften your heart so you can receive His direction at all times.

Sanctification of the Soul

So get rid of all uncleanness and the rampant
outgrowth of wickedness, and in a humble (gentle,
modest) spirit receive and welcome the Word which
implanted and rooted [in your hearts] contains the
power to save your souls.

JAMES 1:21

Once you are born again, your spirit has been reborn and you will go to heaven when you die. But God is not finished—He is just beginning. You need to "work out your own salvation with fear and trembling" (Philippians 2:12 KJV). In other words, your soul needs to be saved. The soul is often defined as the mind, the will, and the emotions. Each of these areas needs salvation.

The Holy Spirit works relentlessly to transform the whole man into God's perfect will. This process is called sanctification. When your soul is renewed with His Word, you think His thoughts and not your own. Submit yourself to the Holy Spirit and allow Him to change every thought and motive.

Resist Rejection

If God is for us, who [can be] against us? [Who can be our foe, if God is on our side?]

ROMANS 8:31

Do you feel as though the world is against you? Does it seem that no matter how hard you try no one is pleased? Maybe you have conflict with a family member. Perhaps your boss finds fault with your work.

Sooner or later you will experience some form of rejection. Not everybody will like you. Some may even aggressively dislike you. No one enjoys being rejected, but you can learn to handle rejection and get on with your life if you remember that Jesus was also rejected and despised. If you feel rejected, give your hurt to God:

Lord, I can't please everyone all of the time. I will concentrate on being a God pleaser and not a man pleaser. The rest I leave in Your hands, Lord. Grant me favor with You and with men, and continue transforming me into the image of Your Son. Thank You, Lord.

Play Your Part

So they came to John and reported to him, Rabbi,
the Man Who was with you on the other side of the
Jordan . . . notice, here He is baptizing too, and
everybody is flocking to Him!

JOHN 3:26

John the Baptist came to prepare the way for the Lord. That was his purpose on earth and he knew it. But John's disciples tried to incite him to jealousy over Jesus' ministry! John replied, "A man must be content to receive the gift which is given him from heaven; there is no other source" (John 3:27).

You have a unique role in the body of Christ. There is no point in being jealous of someone else's spiritual gifts or ministry. God is the only source for gifts and His plan is perfect for each of us. If your gift is giving, then give with zeal. If your gift is helping, then help somebody! Rather than worrying about what others are doing, figure out what God wants and go do it!

An Attitude of Gratitude

Rejoice in the Lord always [delight, gladden
yourselves in Him]; again I say, Rejoice! Let all men
know and perceive and recognize your unselfishness
(your considerateness, your forbearing spirit) . . . Do
not fret or have any anxiety about anything, but in
every circumstance and in everything, by prayer and
petition (definite requests), with thanksgiving,
continue to make your wants known to God.

PHILIPPIANS 4:4-6

We all need to develop an "attitude of gratitude." This doesn't mean we should live pretending nothing negative exists. It simply means we make it our goal in life to be as positive as possible. A positive approach opens the door for God to work.

Go to bed tonight pondering everything you have to be thankful for. Do the same first thing to-morrow morning. Thank God for everything—a convenient parking place; the fact you can walk, see, or hear; your children. Don't become discouraged with yourself when you fall short, and don't quit. Keep at it until you have developed new habits.

Encourage Yourself in the Lord

*David was greatly distressed, for the men spoke of
stoning him because the souls of them all were
bitterly grieved, each man for his sons and
daughters. But David encouraged and
strengthened himself in the Lord his God.*

1 SAMUEL 30:6

When David found himself in a seemingly hopeless situation with no one to support him, he encouraged and strengthened himself in the Lord. Later on, that situation was totally turned around (see 1 Samuel 30:1-20).

If you don't believe in yourself, who is going to? God believes in you, and it is a good thing too; otherwise, you might never make any progress. You cannot always wait for someone else to come along and encourage you to be all you can be. Confidence is something you decide to have. You learn about God—about His love, His ways, and His Word—then ultimately you must decide whether you believe it or not. You will not go forward until you decide to believe in God and yourself.

Possess the Land

The Lord our God said to us in Horeb, You have
dwelt long enough on this mountain . . . Behold, I
have set the land before you; go in and take possession
of the land which the Lord swore to your fathers, to
Abraham, to Isaac, and to Jacob, to give to them and
their descendants after them.

DEUTERONOMY 1:6,8

In Deuteronomy 1:2, Moses pointed out to the Israelites that it was only an eleven-day journey to the border of Canaan (the promised land), yet it had taken them forty years to get there. Forty years is long enough on any mountain! We shouldn't judge the Israelites harshly, because we do the same thing they did. We keep going around and around the same mountains instead of making progress. The result is it takes us years to experience victory over something that could have been dealt with quickly.

Have you spent forty years trying to make an eleven-day trip? Leave the old bondage behind and make up your mind you will not quit until you have taken possession of your rightful inheritance.

Unshakeable Peace

And God's peace [shall be yours, that tranquil state of a soul assured of its salvation through Christ, and so fearing nothing from God and being content with its earthly lot of whatever sort that is, that peace] which transcends all understanding shall garrison and mount guard over your hearts and minds in Christ Jesus.

PHILIPPIANS 4:7

Even in these confusing and frightening times, God wants you to lead an abundant life. Peace and joy and the other fruit of the Spirit are given to you to draw on all the time. When you work on developing fruit in the good times, you have a reserve for difficult times. Mature Christians know how to draw on the peace that can only come from the Prince of Peace who lives inside them.

As a child of God, you need to know how to be steady and stable no matter what the circumstances. Allow His peace to guard your heart and mind so you are prepared to handle times of crisis when they come.

No Regrets

*For godly grief and the pain God is permitted to
direct, produce a repentance that leads and
contributes to salvation and deliverance from evil,
and it never brings regret; but worldly grief (the
hopeless sorrow that is characteristic of the pagan
world) is deadly [breeding and ending in death].*

2 CORINTHIANS 7:10

Regret is ruining the lives of countless people by stealing their joy. Certainly you have things you wish you had done differently. But there is no sense becoming burdened with regret over something you have no power to change. You need to understand this is the way the devil works. God will warn you so you can change your mind before you make a mistake. Satan waits until it's too late, when you can no longer do anything about it, and then tries to heap regret and condemnation upon you.

Don't allow Satan to steal from you any longer. Ask God for forgiveness, if you haven't already, and leave your regrets in the past.

The Right Words

*Nor shall your name any longer be Abram [high,
exalted father]; but your name shall be Abraham
[father of a multitude], for I have made you the father
of many nations . . . As for Sarai your wife, you shall
not call her name Sarai; but Sarah [Princess] her name
shall be. And I will bless her and give you a son also by
her. Yes, I will bless her, and she shall be a mother of
nations; kings of peoples shall come from her.*

GENESIS 17:5,15-16

God gave Abram and Sarai new names
that carried significant meaning. Each time
their names were called, the future was prophesied:
Abraham would be father of a multitude and his prin-
cess, Sarah, would be a mother of nations and kings.

Now the right things were spoken over Abram and
Sarai. Words proclaimed in the natural realm reached
into the realm of the spirit where their miracle was.
Those words came into agreement with God's Word
and called forth the miracle God had promised.

Words are containers for power. Carefully watch
over your words and walk through life with abundant joy!

Tests and Trials

*For no temptation (no trial regarded as enticing to
sin), [no matter how it comes or where it leads] . . .
[has come to you that is beyond human resistance and
that is not adjusted and adapted and belonging to
human experience, and such as man can bear]. But
God is faithful [to His Word and to His compassion-
ate nature], and He [can be trusted] not to let you be
tempted and tried and assayed beyond your ability
and strength of resistance and power to endure, but
with the temptation He will [always] also provide the
way out (the means of escape to a landing place),
that you may be capable and strong and powerful to
bear up under it patiently.*

I CORINTHIANS 10:13

Hard times can bring the temptation to
give up and become negative, depressed,
and angry with God. Life can be difficult, but God
will always intervene and His help will always arrive
on time. Tonight, purpose in your heart to keep pressing on and rest in His presence. God has promised to
deliver you before it is too late!

Hope in God

*Why are you cast down, O my inner self? And why
should you moan over me and be disquieted within
me? Hope in God and wait expectantly for Him, for I
shall yet praise Him, my Help and my God.*

PSALM 42:5

Discouragement destroys hope, so naturally the devil always tries to discourage
you. Without hope you give up, which is what Satan
wants you to do. The Bible repeatedly tells you not
to be discouraged or dismayed. God knows you will
not come through to victory if you get discouraged—He wants you to be encouraged, not discouraged.

When discouragement or condemnation tries to
overtake you, ask the Lord for strength and courage.
Tomorrow is a new day. God loves you and His
mercy is new every morning. Say, "I refuse to be discouraged. Father, the Bible says You love me. You
sent Jesus to die for me. I'll be fine—tomorrow will
be a great day." Hope in Him!

A Spiritual Sabbath

Let us therefore be zealous and exert ourselves and
strive diligently to enter that rest [of God, to know
and experience it for ourselves], that no one may fall
or perish by the same kind of unbelief and disobedi-
ence [into which those in the wilderness fell].

HEBREWS 4:11

If you read the entire fourth chapter of the book of Hebrews, you will find it speaking about a Sabbath rest that is available to God's people. Under the Old Covenant, the Sabbath was observed as a day of rest. Under the New Covenant, this Sabbath rest spoken of is a spiritual place of rest. It is the privilege of every believer to refuse to worry or have anxiety. As a believer, you can enter the rest of God.

The only way to enter that rest is through believing. You will forfeit it through unbelief and disobedience. Unbelief will keep you in the wilderness, but Jesus has provided a permanent place of rest that can be inhabited exclusively through living by faith.

Start Where You Are

Do not say to your neighbor, Go, and come again;
and tomorrow I will give it.

PROVERBS 3:28

When God tells you to help someone, it's easy to put it off. You intend to obey God; it is just that you are going to do it later—when you have more money, when you're not so busy, when Christmas is over, when the kids are back in school, or when vacation is over.

There is no point in praying for God to give you money so you can be a blessing to others if you are not being a blessing with what you already have. Satan will try to tell you that you don't have anything to give—but don't believe Him.

Even if it is only small amounts of money, a pack of gum or a ballpoint pen, start using what you have. As you begin giving what you have, God will bring increase into your life and you will be able to give on an even larger scale.

Bless and Be Blessed by Loving

*But earnestly desire and zealously cultivate the
greatest and best gifts and graces (the higher gifts
and the choicest graces). And yet I will show you a
still more excellent way [one that is better by far and
the highest of them all—love].*

I CORINTHIANS 12:31

Love should be number one on your spiritual priority list. You should learn about love, pray about love, and develop love by loving others.

God is love, so when you walk in His love you abide in Him, He is present. Because we walk in God's love by receiving and expressing it, we should not deceive ourselves into thinking we can love God while we hate other people (see 1 John 4:20).

We seek many things in the course of our lifetime hoping to find fulfillment. But most of these things disappoint. When we decide to walk in love we discover it not only blesses others, it also blesses us.

Calm Down and Use Your Gifts

Peace I leave with you; My [own] peace I now give
and bequeath to you.

Do you know there's a right and wrong way to handle times of distress? I didn't know that until I became a Christian and began to learn that God's power and peace are available to me.

As a Christian, you have God's peace. He has bequeathed it to you—it is your inheritance. In addition, Luke 10:19 tells you He has given you power. Peace and power, what wonderful gifts . . . and God gave them to you for a reason—He wants you to use them.

If you haven't been putting these gifts to work in your life you're cheating yourself. So make a decision to start using them now. Don't waste your time whining, crying, or throwing a fit when problems come. Instead, calm down and think about the peace and power of God that are yours . . . and then put them to work!

Choose Life

I call heaven and earth to witness this day against
you that I have set before you life and death, the
blessings and the curses; therefore choose life, that you
and your descendants may live.

DEUTERONOMY 30:19

Happiness and joy do not come from the outside but from within you. They are the result of a conscious decision, a deliberate choice— one we make each day.

There are many people living in bad situations they would like to see changed. But despite the challenges they choose to be happy and joyous. You face that same choice every day of your life.

Either you choose to passively listen to the devil and allow him to ruin your life and make you miserable, or you choose to aggressively withstand him so you can live in the fullness of life God provided for you through His Son Jesus Christ.

Make the right choice and enjoy life like never before!

Make Love a Habit

And let us consider and give attentive, continuous
care to watching over one another, studying how we
may stir up (stimulate and incite) to love and helpful
deeds and noble activities.

HEBREWS 10:24

If you intend to make love a habit, you must develop the habit of loving people with your words. Your fleshly (lower, sensual) nature points out flaws, weaknesses, and failures. It seems to feed on the negatives in life. It sees and magnifies all that is wrong with people and things. But the Bible says you are to overcome evil with good (see Romans 12:21).

Walking in the Spirit—continually following the leading, guiding, and working of the Holy Spirit through your own spirit instead of being led by your emotions—requires being positive.

It is easy to find something wrong with everyone. But love does not expose faults—it covers them. Ask God to help you share His love with others.

Be a Believer, Not an Achiever

Are you so foolish and so senseless and so silly?
Having begun [your new life spiritually] with the
[Holy] Spirit, are you now reaching perfection [by
dependence] on the flesh?

GALATIANS 3:3

Trying to make things happen on your own without God's help is foolish and often causes feelings of frustration and condemnation. It makes no sense for you to try to do what only God can do.

God wants you to realize it is impossible for you to change yourself—only He can do that through the marvelous wonder of His grace, which is a free gift to everyone who will receive it.

If you have been struggling to achieve good results on your own it's time to make a change. God wants you to struggle less and believe more. Accept the free gift of God's grace and allow Him to change your life into the peaceful, abundant life He has planned for you.

Be Led by Peace

*And let the peace (soul harmony which comes)
from Christ rule (act as umpire continually) in your
hearts [deciding and settling with finality all questions that arise in your minds].*

COLOSSIANS 3:15

The umpire in a baseball game decides whether you are in or out. Peace in your heart should be the umpire that decides whether something should be out of your life, or allowed to remain.

Many people do not enjoy peace because they are out of the will of God. They follow their own will rather than God's will. They do what they feel like or what they think is right rather than following God's Word and being led by peace.

I've learned something can sound good, feel good, and even be a good thing . . . but if I don't have peace about it, I need to leave it alone.

If you want to be sensitive to God's leading, learn to follow peace!

Experience Joy as a Calm Delight

I have told you these things, that My joy and delight may be in you, and that your joy and gladness may be of full measure and complete and overflowing.

JOHN 15:11

Are you like some believers who think that in order to be filled with the joy of the Lord they must be turned on, fired up, and superhyped?

God wants your joy to be full and complete, but that doesn't mean you have to swing from chandeliers!

Some define *joy* as "hilarity," and there is some basis for that definition. But according to *Strong's Concordance*, the Greek word *chara*, translated *joy* in the above verse, means "calm delight."

My husband, Dave, likens this calm delight to a bubbling brook that just flows along quietly and peacefully, bringing refreshment to everything and everyone along its path. Doesn't that sound appealing?

Of course there will be times when your joy will be supercharged and exciting, but most of the time we will live with a simple "calm delight."

Refuse to Be Confused

God is not the author of confusion, but of peace.
1 CORINTHIANS 14:33 KJV

Are you confused? Is there something happening in your life right now you don't understand? Or perhaps you're baffled about the way things happened in your past.

Many people today suffer tremendously with confusion, but that was never God's plan. He doesn't cause your confusion—He wants to stop it.

He doesn't want you to try to figure out everything that happens in your life. He knows what is going on and why, and He is in control.

That means you don't have to worry and live in confusion. It almost sounds too easy, but you can have total freedom from the torment of confusion just by refusing the temptation to figure things out. So trust God to take care of everything that concerns you and enjoy a peaceful, happy life.

Rejoice in Today

*This is the day which the Lord hath made; we will
rejoice and be glad in it.*

PSALM 118:24 KJV

The Lord once told me anxiety is caused by trying to mentally and emotionally get into things that are not here yet or that have already passed—mentally leaving today and getting into an area of the past or the future.

Since then I have been trying to learn to lighten up and enjoy life. I try to live life one day at a time and not worry about the past or future. We need to be responsible, but we also need to relax and take things as they come without getting all nervous and upset.

Learn to enjoy the good life God provided for you. In spite of all the troubling things going on in the world, make this daily confession: "This is the day the Lord has made, and I will rejoice and be glad in it."

Don't Fret—Rejoice!

Rejoice in the Lord always . . . again I say,
Rejoice! . . . Do not fret or have any anxiety about
anything, but in . . . everything, by prayer and
petition, . . . with thanksgiving, continue to
make your wants known to God.

PHILIPPIANS 4:4,6

Twice in this passage the apostle Paul tells us to rejoice. He urges us not to fret or have any anxiety about anything but to pray and give thanks to God in everything—not after everything is over.

If you wait until everything is perfect before rejoicing and giving thanks you won't have much fun. Learning to enjoy life even in the midst of trying circumstances is one way to develop spiritual maturity.

Live in the fullness of the joy of the Lord by finding something to be glad about besides your current circumstances. You must learn to derive your happiness and joy from the Lord who lives inside you.

Decide you will not fret or have anxiety about anything but will give thanks and praise to God, rejoicing in Him always.

Accept God's Great Grace

But where sin increased and abounded, grace
(God's unmerited favor) has surpassed it and
increased the more and superabounded.

ROMANS 5:20

God conquers evil with good by pouring out His limitless grace upon you so that if you sin, His grace becomes greater than your sin. God's love is the power that forgives your sins, heals your emotional wounds, and mends your broken heart.

Once you realize you are loved by God—not because of anything you are or anything you have done—you can quit trying to earn His love and simply receive and enjoy it.

Start by confessing aloud several times a day that God loves you. Speak it out and get comfortable with the thought of it. Bask in His love and let it saturate your soul. Once your heart is filled with the knowledge of God's love you can begin to love Him in return: We love Him because He first loved us.

Enjoy Your Inheritance

*In Him we also were made [God's] heritage . . .
and we obtained an inheritance . . . so that we who
first hoped in Christ [who first put our confidence in
Him have been destined and appointed to] live for the
praise of His glory!*

EPHESIANS 1:11-12

As a believer, you are meant to enjoy your spiritual inheritance. Life presents many challenges, but you must recognize what is rightfully yours through placing your confidence in Christ. You don't have to live on an emotional roller coaster, feeling up one day and down the next. Instead, you can live as Christ lived, with a sense of peace and security that comes from knowing who you are and whose you are.

Until you make the decision to claim and live in your inheritance, the enemy will continue to rob you of what Jesus died to provide you—His righteousness, peace, and joy that prevail even in the midst of turmoil and confusion.

So calm down, cheer up, and learn to enjoy the inheritance that is yours through Christ.

Simplify Your Life

*You were wearied with the length of your way [in
trying to find rest and satisfaction in alliances apart
from the true God], yet you did not say, There is no
result or profit.*

ISAIAH 57:10

There seems to be a great lack of simplicity in society today, even among Christians. Somehow life gets so complicated it eventually
drains you of your energy and produces frustration
and fatigue.

One translation of the first line of this verse
from Isaiah is, "You are wearied out through the
multiplicity of your ways." The answer for the problem of multiplicity is a return to simplicity.

In our modern society, we think that more is always better. But the writer of Ecclesiastes warns that
the more your goods increase, the more complicated your life becomes (see Ecclesiastes 5:11-12).

Instead of making everything so difficult, why
don't you decide to simplify your life and enjoy the
rest and satisfaction that comes through following
God's plan?

Have an Attitude of Faith

*Faith is the assurance . . . of the things [we] hope
for, being the proof of things [we] do not see.*

HEBREWS 11:1

Faith can be described in many ways, but a very simple way to look at faith—even to examine whether or not you are operating in it— is to say that "faith has an attitude."

Hebrews 4 says that those who have believed God—those who have an attitude of faith—enter His rest and cease from the weariness and pain of human labors.

The attitude of faith does not worry, fret, or have anxiety concerning tomorrow, because faith understands that wherever it needs to go, even into the unknowns of the future, Jesus has already been there.

Remember, He is the Alpha and the Omega. Not only is He the Beginning and the End, He is everything in between. So have an attitude of faith as you pray tonight, placing your trust completely in the one who was, who is, and who is to come.

Exchange Ashes for Beauty

[Cast] all your care upon him; for he careth for you.

1 PETER 5:7 KJV

Do you know God wants to take care of you? It's true. He wants you to give Him all your cares, your problems, your failures—your "ashes"—and in exchange He will give you beauty.

Many people want God to take care of them, but they continue worrying or trying to figure out the answers to their problems instead of waiting for His direction. They continue to wallow in their "ashes" and expect God to give them beauty. But it doesn't work that way—God can only give you beauty when you give Him the ashes.

It's a great privilege to be cared for by the King of kings, so give up your worries and concerns to Him and enjoy His protection, stability, and fullness of joy.

Are You Lovable?

*God shows and clearly proves His [own] love for us
by the fact that while we were still sinners, Christ (the
Messiah, the Anointed One) died for us.*

ROMANS 5:8

When you read the title on this page—
Are You Lovable?—you may have immediately thought, "No, I'm not!"

I would have probably responded the same way
before I came to understand the true nature of God's
love and His reason for loving me.

How can God love you as imperfect as you are?
He loves you because He wants to. It pleases Him.
God loves you because that is His nature. God is love
(see 1 John 4:8). If He were otherwise, He wouldn't
be who He is.

God may not always love everything you do, but
He does love you. His love is unconditional—it is
based on Him, not you.

Live According to God's Plan

Cursed [with great evil] is the strong man who trusts in and relies on frail man, making weak [human] flesh his arm, and whose mind and heart turn aside from the Lord.

JEREMIAH 17:5

The Bible speaks of the arm of the flesh and the arm of the Lord. One is based on human ideas and effort; the other is based on God's plan and power.

It is hard work to carry out the plans and schemes you yourself devise because you are operating in the flesh. But when God starts something, He carries it through to completion without any struggle on your part.

If you are facing struggles, it may be because you are taking matters into your own hands instead of being patient and waiting on the Lord to work things out according to His perfect will.

So stop struggling—turn away from the arm of the flesh and learn to live victoriously according to God's divine plan and purpose for your life.

Succeed at Being Yourself

The [Holy] Spirit . . . bears us up in our weakness.

ROMANS 8:26

Are you tired of playing games, wearing masks, and trying to be someone other than who you are? Wouldn't you like the freedom just to be accepted as you are, without pressure to be someone you really don't know how to be? Would you like to learn how to succeed at being yourself?

God wants you to accept yourself, to like who you are, and to learn to deal with your weaknesses. Everyone has weaknesses, but God doesn't want you to reject yourself because of them.

If you base your value on your weaknesses, you will underestimate your value. Your worth is not based on anything you do but on what God has already done.

So if the devil has been trying to convince you that you don't measure up to the proper standard, remind him tonight that everyone is imperfect and that God loves you just the way you are.

Give Away What You Have

*Beloved, if God loved us so [very much], we also
ought to love one another.*

1 JOHN 4:11

What a blessing it is to have God's love in
you—but you must not hoard it for
yourself. God wants you to give it away . . . to love
others lavishly and unconditionally as He has loved
you.

Everyone in the world desires to be loved and
accepted. God's love is the most wonderful gift He
could give you. And you have the privilege of sharing that love by allowing it to flow through you into
the lives of others.

Many people try to find happiness in getting, but
true happiness can only be found in giving. Think of
yourself as a dispensary of blessings. Be the kind of
person others come to looking for love and blessings. You'll discover that as you give love away, you'll
reap happiness and love in your own life.

Isn't it comforting to know you are lovable?
Now share your love with someone else.

Little Things Mean a Lot

For who has despised the day of small things?
ZECHARIAH 4:10 NKJV

Little things are often viewed as being insignificant, but in reality they are very important. They are the spice of life.

It is a mistake to be interested only in the main course (big things), disregarding the need for the little things (spices). The main course without spice is bland, tasteless, and unsatisfying.

Parents may feel they are showing love for their family by working long hours and bringing home plenty of money to assure financial security. But if working long hours and making lots of money (the seemingly big thing) means they have little time at home for the little things like talking and laughing with the family and doing fun things together, the marriage and family relationships become dull and unsatisfying.

So if you've been overlooking the importance of the little things in life, it's time to add some spice to your life. Why not start tonight?

Freedom from the Pit

I waited patiently and expectantly for the Lord;
and He inclined to me and heard my cry. He drew me up
out of a horrible pit . . . and set my feet upon a rock.

PSALM 40:1-2

When the Bible speaks of "the pit," I always think of the depths of depression.

David spoke of feeling as though he were in a pit, calling out to the Lord to rescue him and set his feet on solid ground.

Nobody wants to be in the pit of depression. Satan takes advantage of your situation by reminding you of painful memories.

When you are depressed, the devil's goal is to make you so miserable and hopeless you will never rise up to cause him any problems or to fulfill the call of God on your life.

So if you're struggling in a pit that keeps you from being all God wants you to be, cry out to the Lord and allow Him to draw you out of the pit and set you free. God has a great life planned for you, don't let Satan steal it through depression.

Eliminate the Negative

The communication of thy faith may become effectual by the acknowledging of every good thing which is in you in Christ Jesus.

PHILEMON 1:6 KJV

The communication of your faith is made effectual by acknowledging every good thing that is in you through Christ Jesus, not by acknowledging every thing that is wrong with you.

The devil wants you to spend every waking moment acknowledging in your mind and out of your mouth how awful you are. He continually tries to redirect your focus from who you are in Christ, back to your shortcomings. He wants to deceive you into believing that because of your faults, you are worthless.

But you can increase your self-acceptance and improve your opinion of yourself by deciding right here and now you will not entertain one more negative thought or allow one more negative word about yourself to come out of your mouth.

Start acknowledging the good things that are in you because of Christ.

There Is a Way Out

We are hedged in (pressed) on every side
[troubled and oppressed in every way], but not
cramped or crushed; we suffer embarrassments and are
perplexed and unable to find a way out,
but not driven to despair.

2 CORINTHIANS 4:8

Despair is a state in which a person feels so overcome by a sense of futility or defeat they don't know what to do. At such times it seems there is no way out. But for believers there is always a way out of every situation because Jesus has told us, "I am the Way" (John 14:6).

It is very comforting to know that although there are times when you are pressed on every side and perplexed because there seems to be no way out, the Lord has promised He will not forsake you.

So when it seems you've come to a dead end, don't be driven to despair. God will show you the way to go and lead you through to victory.

Let the Master Builder Complete the Job

*For [of course] every house is built and
furnished by someone, but the Builder of all
things and the Furnisher [of the entire
equipment of all things] is God.*

HEBREWS 3:4

God is the Master Builder—the one who builds and equips you for the work of the Lord Jesus Christ. The Bible tells you it is God who starts a good work in you, and it is God who will finish it!

This means you should let Him do His work in you. There are certain things only God can do, and your part is to let Him do it. You are to handle your responsibility but cast your care on Him.

Confess your sins and failures to the Lord, confident that He will forgive you. Then trust Him with the job of perfecting you for the work He wants you to do in this life. This will take the pressure off of you and relieve you of the anxiety of trying to perfect yourself.

Have No Fear

There is no fear in love; but perfect love casteth out fear: because fear hath torment. He that feareth is not made perfect in love.

1 JOHN 4:18 KJV

Have you ever started to step out in faith and, even at the thought of it, felt fear rising up in you? It happens to everyone, but it is important to realize that the source of fear is Satan.

Satan doesn't want you to do what God wants you to do and receive all God has for you, so he sends fear to try to torment you into being doubtful and miserable. Fear is an evil spirit that hinders progress.

But you can live without fear by building your faith on what God has said in His Word. There is great power in confessing the Word of God.

So when Satan attempts to torment you with fear, confess what the Word says—that the Lord is with you and "will not fail you or forsake you" (Deuteronomy 31:6). Take steps of faith even if you have to "do it afraid."

Do It Afraid!

The Lord said to Abram, Go . . . away from your country, from your relatives and your father's house, to the land that I will show you.

GENESIS 12:1

How would you feel if God told you to leave your home, your family, and everything that is familiar and comfortable and head out to who knows where?

That is the challenge Abram faced, and it frightened him. But God kept saying to him, "Fear not." That's the same message He gave to Joshua when He called him to lead the children of Israel to the promised land.

You want to wait until you're not afraid before you do anything, but if you do that, you will accomplish very little for God. Abram and Joshua had to step out in faith and obedience to do what God had commanded them to do—and they had to do it afraid. They took "steps of faith" even though they had "feelings of fear."

That's what you will have to do to accomplish the job God wants you to do. But He'll be with you, saying, "Fear not."

You Are Not of This World

*These are [still] in the world . . . [but] they are
not of the world . . . just as I am not of the
world . . . Keep and protect them from the evil one.*

JOHN 17:11,14-15

People in the world are under such intense pressure they are often hurried,
rude, short-tempered, and frustrated. They experience financial and marital stress and the stress of
raising children in a changing and uncertain world.
Because of mental stress on the job and physical
stress from overwork and frayed nerves, some people
seem to be time bombs on the verge of explosion.

As a believer, you do not need to succumb to the
stress that affects people who do not know Jesus as
their Savior. You do not have to operate in the world's
system.

God has provided ways for you to live in the
world without being affected by that type of stress.
Jesus is the Prince of Peace, and following the leading of the Holy Spirit will always lead you to peace
and joy, not to anxiety and frustration.

Refuse to Lose

Behold, the Lord thy God hath set the land
before thee: go up and possess it, as the Lord God
of thy fathers hath said unto thee; fear not, neither
be discouraged.

DEUTERONOMY 1:21 KJV

All of us become disappointed when we have plans that fail, hopes that don't materialize, and goals that are not reached. When this continues for a while, we become discouraged, a condition that can lead to depression if not handled properly.

When you get discouraged, you must make a decision to adapt and adjust, to take a new approach, to just keep going despite your feelings. That's when you must remember the Greater One resides within you and decide you won't let discouragement keep you from realizing your dreams and goals.

When you feel discouraged it is sometimes difficult to be positive. That's when you must rise above the discouragement through Him who lives in you. He is always available to help you find renewed direction and hope. I always say, "When you're discouraged, get encouraged, and when you're disappointed, get reappointed."

Are You Lonely Tonight?

For I will turn their mourning into joy and will comfort them and make them rejoice after their sorrow.

JEREMIAH 31:13

One of the many sources of sorrow is loneliness. Some who suffer most from loneliness, which is a form of grief, are the shy or extremely timid; those who feel misunderstood; the divorced and unmarried; the widowed; the elderly . . . the list goes on and on.

Loneliness can manifest as an inner ache, a vacuum, or a craving for affection. Its side effects include feelings of emptiness, uselessness, or purposelessness. But loneliness can be cured, no matter what the cause.

If you are lonely, you must realize you can confront it in the name of Jesus Christ.

God has promised to be with you always and to never leave or forsake you. Ask Him to reveal His precious Presence to you. Also, ask Him for what I call "divine connections"—right friends who will be real friends that God Himself has chosen for you. Stand on His promise that He will comfort you and cause you to rejoice. Then get ready for the joy!

Be Willing and Yielded

If God is for us, who [can be] against us? [Who can be our foe, if God is on our side?]

ROMANS 8:31

You do not have to depend on your own human efforts to overcome adversity and opposition or to earn favor and win promotion. When God is ready to move in your life, He will give you favor and promotion—and no devil in hell or person on earth will be able to prevent it from happening.

It doesn't matter what people think of you. Your weaknesses and inabilities don't make any difference to God. His criteria for using people is not their talents, gifts, and abilities. He is looking for people who are willing and yielded. God looks for availability, not ability.

Let God build you, your reputation, and your career. When the time is right He will deliver you out of adversity, and then you'll see the fulfillment of your dreams.

Honor Him First

But as for you, the anointing (the sacred appointment, the unction) which you received from Him abides [permanently] in you; [so] then you have no need that anyone should instruct you.

1 JOHN 2:27

This verse isn't suggesting you don't need anyone to teach you the Word. Otherwise God wouldn't appoint some to teach in the body of Christ. But it does say if you are in Christ you have an anointing that abides on the inside of you to guide and direct your life.

Sometimes you give more consideration to what people tell you than to what God has said. You might occasionally ask somebody for their wisdom, but if you hear from God and then start asking everybody else what they think, you are honoring people's opinions above the Word of God. You need to say, "God, no matter what anybody else says, no matter what my own plan is, if You say something to me, I am going to honor You above anything else."

Seek the Truth

*The sower sows the Word. The ones along the path
are those who have the Word sown [in their hearts],
but when they hear, Satan comes at once and [by
force] takes away the message which is sown in them.*

MARK 4:14-15

If you hear or study the Word, the devil
will immediately attempt to steal it from
you. He does not want the Word to take root in
your heart and begin to produce good fruit in your
life. When you learn the truth, deception is uncov-
ered and you are set free. Satan hates and fears the
Word. He will do anything possible to prevent you
from learning God's Word.

The reason Satan works so hard to keep you
from the Word is simple: he knows the Word of
God is a powerful weapon against him. It assures his
defeat! That is why it is imperative that you learn to
wield the spiritual sword. Reading, hearing, believing, meditating on, and confessing the Word cancels
Satan's evil plan. Tonight, determine to make the
Word of God a priority in your life.

Little by Little

But we do [strongly and earnestly] desire for each of you to show the same diligence and sincerity [all the way through] in realizing and enjoying the full assurance and development of [your] hope until the end.

HEBREWS 6:11

In some ways, spiritual growth can be compared to physical growth. Sadly, many people do not enjoy their children while they are raising them. At each stage of growth the parents wish the child was in another stage. If the child is crawling, they wish he was walking, out of diapers, in school, getting married, and on and on.

In Deuteronomy 7:22, Moses told the children of Israel the Lord would drive out their enemies before them "little by little." Between each victory in your life there is a time of waiting, but it is usually difficult because you want everything now! As a Christian you grow throughout your lifetime and never stop progressing. Learn to enjoy each stage of life as it comes because each has joys uniquely its own.

Dream Big Dreams

*Through skillful and godly Wisdom is a house (a
life, a home, a family) built, and by understanding it
is established [on a sound and good foundation]. And
by knowledge shall its chambers [of every area] be
filled with all precious and pleasant riches.*

PROVERBS 24:3-4

Do you have a dream or a vision in your
heart for something greater than what
you have now? Ephesians 3:20 tells us God is able to
do exceedingly abundantly above and beyond all we
can hope, ask, or think. If you are not thinking, hoping, or asking—you are cheating yourself. You need
to think big thoughts, dream big dreams, and ask for
big things.

There is a gold mine of dreams, visions, abilities, and strength hidden in every life, but you have
to dig to get to it. You must be willing to dig deep
and go beyond how you feel or what is convenient.
If you will dig down deep into the spirit, you will do
greater things than anyone could ever imagine.

An Effective Prayer

*And when you pray, do not heap up phrases
(multiply words, repeating the same ones over and
over) as the Gentiles do, for they think they will be
heard for their much speaking.*

MATTHEW 6:7

Too often we get caught up in our own works concerning prayer. Sometimes we try to pray so long, loud, and fancy that we lose sight of the fact that prayer is simply conversation with God. The length or loudness or eloquence of our prayer is not the issue—it is the sincerity of our heart and our faith God hears that is important.

We must develop simple, believing prayer. We need the confidence that even if we only say, "God, help me," He hears and will answer. We should believe that God wants to help us because He is our Helper (see Hebrews 13:6). We can depend on God to be faithful to do what we have asked Him to do, as long as our request is in accordance with His will.

Run On Through

Let us strip off and throw aside every encumbrance
(unnecessary weight) and that sin which so readily
(deftly and cleverly) clings to and entangles us, and
let us run with patient endurance and steady and
active persistence the appointed course of the race
that is set before us.

HEBREWS 12:1

When you begin your journey to whole-ness with the Lord, you are usually all knotted up inside. As you allow Him to do so, He begins to straighten up your life by untying one knot at a time. The temptation is to run away from your problems, but the Lord says that you are to go through them.

The good news is that Jesus has promised that you will never have to go through them alone. He will always be there to help you in every way. He said, "I am the way, follow Me." When you decide to follow Jesus, you will soon learn He never turns back in fear. His path is always straightforward to the finish line.

These Perilous Times

*But understand this, that in the last days will come
(set in) perilous times of great stress and trouble [hard
to deal with and hard to bear]. For people will be
lovers of self and [utterly] self-centered, lovers of
money and aroused by an inordinate [greedy] desire for
wealth, proud and arrogant and contemptuous boast-
ers. They will be abusive (blasphemous, scoffing),
disobedient to parents, ungrateful, unholy and profane.*

2 TIMOTHY 3:1-2

Just as Paul predicted long ago, these are
perilous times. There has now arisen a
new generation of people, many of whom have not
been taught anything about God in school, nor have
they been taught to pray at home. They have seen
some sad examples of spiritual leaders who have
publicly fallen, and having no solid foundation, it is
easy for them to conclude that "religion" is a bunch
of junk.

As a believer, you must strive to be different than
the world. Be a good example. Walk in love, being
honorable in all your conduct. People are watching
you. Show them that Christ lives in you.

Why Worry?

Cease from anger and forsake wrath; fret not
yourself—it tends only to evildoing.

PSALM 37:8

Anxiety and worry are both attacks on the mind intended to keep you from serving the Lord. The enemy uses these weapons to press your faith down so you cannot live in victory. Many people are worriers but don't even realize it. They may call it something else—but it is still worry. In addition to telling you to "fret not," other passages warn you to "take no thought" (Matthew 6:25), "be careful for nothing" (Philippians 4:6), and "cast . . . all your care" (1 Peter 5:7).

Matthew 6:27 says, "And who of you by worrying and being anxious can add one unit of measure (cubit) to his stature or to the span of his life?" The obvious point is that worry is useless. It does not accomplish any good thing. In that case, why worry and why be so anxious?

Praying His Will

[Yes] I will grant [I Myself will do for you]
whatever you shall ask in My Name [as presenting
all that I Am].

JOHN 14:14

Some Christians read this passage and take its meaning out of context. What a statement! Wouldn't it be wonderful if this gave you license to have anything and everything you want? But the name of Jesus is not simply a "magic word" to tack on at the end of your wish list.

You must realize that all effective prayer involves praying the will of God, not the will of man. There are many things in the Word that clearly reveal God's will, and these you may certainly ask for boldly without any hesitation or concern about whether you should have them. Yet there are many other things you need to pray about without knowing the exact will of God in the situation. It is at these times you should pray that His perfect will be done and not your own.

Small Beginnings

Who [with reason] despises the day of small things?
ZECHARIAH 4:10

You are probably believing God for something to come to pass in your life. If you look, you will find evidence of a small beginning. God gives you seed—perhaps only a little, tiny seed—something that causes you to hope. Rejoice over that seed. It is a sign of greater things to come.

When you despise something you regard it lightly. You count it as nothing and don't take care of it. But if you don't take care of what God gives you, you will lose it. You need to be content during the small things. You know the Lord is the Author and the Finisher (see Hebrews 12:2). What He begins, He completes (see Philippians 1:6). Don't curse your seed by complaining or proclaiming negative things over it. Instead say, "Lord, this is only a little thing, but thank You for giving me some hope, something to hold on to. Thank You, Lord, for a beginning."

A Strong Fortress

I will say of the Lord, He is my Refuge and my
Fortress, my God; on Him I lean and rely, and in Him
I [confidently] trust! . . . You shall not be afraid of
the terror of the night, nor of the arrow (the evil
plots and slanders of the wicked) that flies by day, nor
of the pestilence that stalks in darkness, nor of the
destruction and sudden death that surprise and lay
waste at noonday.

PSALM 91:2,5-6

You need to remember you are ready for anything through Christ who infuses inner strength into you. Paul prayed for the Church at Ephesus to be strengthened with all might and power in the inner man (see Ephesians 3:16). He knew if they stayed strong inwardly, they would be able to handle whatever came against them.

When you trust God, you don't have to be afraid of the devil's sudden surprises that stalk you. He is your strong fortress. No matter what may come against you, you will not be defeated.

Hear and Obey

Sacrifice and offering You do not desire, nor have You delight in them; You have given me the capacity to hear and obey [Your law, a more valuable service than] burnt offerings and sin offerings [which] You do not require.

PSALM 40:6

God delights in your obedience. Naturally, it doesn't do Him any good to speak to you if you aren't going to listen and obey. For many years, I wanted God to talk to me, but I wanted to pick and choose what to obey. I wanted to do what He said if I thought it was a good idea. If I didn't like what I was hearing, I would act like it wasn't from God.

Some of what God says will be exciting. Some things might not be so thrilling to hear. But that doesn't mean what He tells you won't work out for good if you will just do it His way. God does not require a higher sacrifice than obedience.

Sufficient Grace

My grace (My favor and loving-kindness and mercy) is enough for you [sufficient against any danger and enables you to bear the trouble manfully]; for My strength and power are made perfect (fulfilled and completed) and show themselves most effective in [your] weakness.

2 CORINTHIANS 12:9

Do you ever wonder why God does not always deliver you from your bondage and problems immediately? The reason is because only the Lord knows everything that needs to be done in the lives of His children—and the perfect timing for it to be done.

You are not always delivered from your distress at the precise moment you call on the name of the Lord. Sometimes you must endure for a while, be patient and continue in faith. Thank God, during those times in which the Lord decides for whatever reason not to deliver you right away, He always gives the grace and strength you need to press on toward eventual victory.

Great Expectations

And therefore the Lord [earnestly] waits [expect-
ing, looking, and longing] to be gracious to you; and
therefore He lifts Himself up, that He may have
mercy on you and show loving-kindness to you. For
the Lord is a God of justice. Blessed (happy, fortu-
nate, to be envied) are all those who [earnestly] wait
for Him, who expect and look and long for Him [for
His victory, His favor, His love, His peace, His joy,
and His matchless, unbroken companionship]!

ISAIAH 30:18

What a wonderful promise. God is earnestly looking for someone to be good
to—but there is one requirement. You must be expecting, looking, and longing for God's goodness.

Hebrews 6:19 says hope is the anchor of the
soul. Hope is the force that keeps you steady in a
time of trial. Don't ever stop hoping. Things may
not always turn out the way you want them to, but
even in disappointing times there is still reason to
hope. Expect a miracle in your life. Expect good
things!

Peculiar Treasure

*Now therefore, if you will obey My voice in truth
and keep My covenant, then you shall be My own
peculiar possession and treasure from among and
above all peoples; for all the earth is Mine. And you
shall be to Me a kingdom of priests, a holy nation
[consecrated, set apart to the worship of God].*

EXODUS 19:5-6

Self-rejection and self-hatred can almost seem pious in a sense. They can become a way of punishing yourself for your mistakes, failures, and inabilities. People cannot be perfect, so they sometimes reject and despise themselves.

Do you lack appreciation for your own worth and value? You may not feel treasured or even acceptable, but you are. In Ephesians 1:6, Paul says that all who believe in Christ have been "accepted in the beloved." What joyous and amazing affirmation! Surely you are valuable; otherwise your heavenly Father would not have paid such a heavy price for your redemption.

Confidence in Christ

Do not, therefore, fling away your fearless
confidence, for it carries a great and glorious
compensation of reward. For you have need of steadfast
patience and endurance, so that you may perform and
fully accomplish the will of God, and thus receive and
carry away [and enjoy to the full] what is promised.

HEBREWS 10:35-36

What is confidence? It has been defined as the quality of assurance that leads one to undertake something; the belief that one is able and acceptable; the certainty that causes one to be bold, open, and plain.

The devil begins his assault on personal confidence wherever he can find an opening, especially during the vulnerable years of childhood. His goal is to undermine the person because an individual without confidence will never fulfill the plan of God for his life.

Christ is in you, ready to help with everything you do for Him. Jesus can restore your confidence and give you the strength, power, and boldness to do what you could never do on your own. Be confident—it is part of your spiritual inheritance!

Seeing in the Darkness

God is faithful (reliable, trustworthy, and therefore ever true to His promise, and He can be depended on); by Him you were called into companionship and participation with His Son, Jesus Christ our Lord.

1 CORINTHIANS 1:9

There are times you just can't see through the darkness that seems to be closing in around you. It is in those times of endurance and patience that your faith is stretched and you learn to trust God even when you can't hear His voice.

You can grow in your confidence level to the point where "knowing" is even better than "hearing." You may not know what to do, but it is sufficient to know the one who does know. Everyone likes specific direction; however, when you don't have it, knowing God is faithful and ever true to His promise, and that He has promised to be with us always, is comforting and keeps us stable until His timing comes to illuminate the situation.

The Lie of Self

For we [Christians] are the true circumcision, who
worship God in spirit and by the Spirit of God and
exult and glory and pride ourselves in Jesus Christ,
and put no confidence or dependence [on what we
are] in the flesh and on outward privileges and
physical advantages and external appearances.

PHILIPPIANS 3:3

Self-confidence is the buzzword of to-day's culture. Society proclaims a basic need to believe in oneself and that you need to feel good if you are ever going to accomplish anything in life. Too many believe that lie.

Many people spend their lives climbing the ladder of success only to reach the top and discover their ladder was propped against the wrong building. Others strive to perform perfectly, only to endure repeated failures. The result is always the same— emptiness and misery.

You don't need to believe in yourself—you need to believe in Jesus in you. You do not need self-confidence. You need God-confidence!

Be Who You Are

Let us not become vainglorious and self-conceited,
competitive and challenging and provoking and
irritating to one another, envying and being jealous
of one another.

GALATIANS 5:26

In Galatians 6:4 the apostle Paul exhorts you to grow in the Lord until you come to the point you can have the personal satisfaction and joy of doing something commendable in itself alone without resorting to boastful comparison with other people.

Thank God, once you know who you are in Christ, you are set free from the stress of comparison and competition. You know you have worth and value apart from your works and accomplishments. Therefore you can do your best to glorify God, rather than just trying to be better than someone else. What a glorious, wonderful freedom to be secure in Christ and not have to be controlled by strife, envy, or jealousy. You can be who God created you to be! He doesn't make mistakes!

From Pit to Palace

When Joseph had come to his brothers, they stripped him of his [distinctive] long garment which he was wearing; Then they took him and cast him into the [well-like] pit which was empty; there was no water in it.

GENESIS 37:23-24

When Joseph's brothers threw him in the pit to die, God had other plans. Scripture says that even though Joseph was sold as a slave, he did not have a slave mentality. He still believed he could do great things. Ultimately he ended up second in command to Pharaoh, the ruler over all Egypt. How did Joseph get from the pit to the palace? It was by remaining positive, refusing to be bitter, being confident, and trusting God.

Make up your mind right now to do something great for God. No matter where you started, you can have a great finish. If people have mistreated you, don't waste your time trying to get revenge—leave them in God's hands and trust Him to bring justice in your life.

The Stress-Free Life

*Come to Me, all you who labor and are heavy-
laden and overburdened, and I will cause you to rest.
[I will ease and relieve and refresh your souls.]*

MATTHEW 11:28

Many people today are stressed out beyond anything a human being was ever
meant to endure. Every person is very different,
uniquely created by God's design. What is complicated for one may be simple for another. Don't compare yourself with other people. But when faced
with a problem or difficult circumstance you must
ask yourself, "What would Jesus have me do in this
situation? How would He handle it?"

Jesus was not stressed out or burned out. He
was not controlled by circumstances or the demands
of other people. In John 14:6, Jesus said, "I am the
Way." His way is the right way—the way that will
lead you into righteousness, peace, and joy. Jesus
prayed that His enjoyment would fill your soul, and
it will when you learn to take His approach to life
and its many different challenges.

No Condemnation

He who believes in Him [who clings to, trusts in,
relies on Him] is not judged [he who trusts in Him
never comes up for judgment; for him there is no rejec-
tion, no condemnation—he incurs no damnation].

JOHN 3:18

The Holy Spirit works to convict you of sin and convince you of righteousness (see John 16:7-11). His conviction is intended to convince you to repent, which means to turn around and go in the right direction.

It is normal to feel guilty when you are initially convicted of sin; but to keep feeling guilty after you have repented is not healthy, nor is it God's will. Conviction is entirely different from condemnation. Condemnation presses you down and puts you under a burden of guilt, but conviction is meant to lift you out of something, to help you move up higher in God's plan for your life. If you are suffering under a burden of condemnation, lay your guilt before the throne of God tonight and receive His forgiveness and mercy.

The Sword of the Spirit

Stand therefore [hold your ground], having tightened the belt of truth around your loins and having put on the breastplate of integrity and of moral rectitude and right standing with God, and having shod your feet in preparation [to face the enemy with the firm-footed stability, the promptness, and the readiness produced by the good news] of the Gospel of peace. Lift up over all the [covering] shield of saving faith, upon which you can quench all the flaming missiles of the wicked [one]. And take the helmet of salvation and the sword that the Spirit wields, which is the Word of God.

EPHESIANS 6:14-17

This passage instructs you to wear armor that serves as protection against the principalities and powers of the enemy. You have defensive armor and a powerful offensive weapon—the sword of the Spirit. A sword kept in the sheath has no value. It must be wielded—taken from the sheath and used. The Word of God is your sword. When Satan attacks your mind say, "It is written" and quote a Scripture that opposes his lie.

The Written Word

Your word is a lamp to my feet
and a light to my path.

PSALM 119:105

The Bible is written as a personal letter to you. God speaks to you, ministers to your needs, and directs you in the way you should go in His written Word. He tells you what you should do and how you should live.

It is a mistake to think we can hear clearly from God without spending time in the Word. Knowing the written Word protects you from deception. Listening for God's voice without being dedicated to spending time in the Word on a regular basis opens you up to hearing voices that are not from God. There may be times when God speaks something to you that is outside a specific chapter and verse of the Bible, but it will always be in agreement with His Word. Tonight, spend time reading a portion of God's personal letter to you and allow Him to speak to your heart. God's Word is one of the most precious gifts we have. Treasure it.

Yearnings in the Night

My soul yearns for You [O Lord] in the night, yes,
my spirit within me seeks You earnestly.

ISAIAH 26:9

Nothing can satisfy your longing for God except communion and fellowship with Him. The apostle John wrote, "And the world passes away and disappears, and with it the forbidden cravings (the passionate desires, the lust) of it; but he who does the will of God and carries out His purposes in his life abides (remains) forever" (1 John 2:17).

The world makes it easy for you to fill your ears with all kinds of things that drown out the voice of God and push Him far into the background of your life. However, the day comes for every person when only God remains. Everything else in life eventually passes away; when it does, God will still be there. Seek God earnestly tonight and He will abide in you.

Tame the Tongue

Look at the ships: though they are so great and are driven by rough winds, they are steered by a very small rudder wherever the impulse of the helmsman determines. Even so the tongue is a little member, and it can boast of great things. . . . But the human tongue can be tamed by no man. It is a restless (undisciplined, irreconcilable) evil, full of deadly poison.

JAMES 3:4-5, 8

Anything undisciplined will be wild and uncontrollable, always wanting to do its own thing. A child is that way. So is a wild animal. So is appetite. The human tongue is no different. No man can tame the tongue—not by himself. You need the Holy Spirit's help, but God will not do it all for you. You must discipline your mouth and take responsibility for what comes out of it.

How do you talk about your future? If you are not satisfied with your life and want to see it change, begin speaking over yourself according to God's Word. Let your words be in agreement with God's Word and you will be blessed greatly.

The Perfect Plan

For I know the thoughts and plans that I have
for you, says the Lord, thoughts and plans for welfare
and peace and not for evil, to give you hope in your
final outcome.

JEREMIAH 29:11

God has a perfect plan for all those who put their faith in Jesus Christ as Lord of their lives. His plan is complete in great detail, and it will lead all who follow Him to an abundant life. But only a few ever enjoy the fulfillment of God's plan because most don't know how to listen to God's leading and follow Him. Instead they choose (either willfully or ignorantly) to go their own way.

You can walk in the perfect will of God if you will learn how to hear from Him and follow His instructions. But listening to Him is your decision. God won't force you to choose His will. However, He will do everything He can to encourage you to say yes to His direction.

Uncommon Wisdom

If any of you is deficient in wisdom, let him ask of
the giving God [Who gives] to everyone liberally and
ungrudgingly, without reproaching or faultfinding,
and it will be given him.

JAMES 1:5

Surprisingly, many sophisticated and intelligent people lack wisdom and common sense. Wisdom and common sense are closely
linked—wisdom discerns truth in a situation, while
common sense provides good judgment regarding
what to do about the truth. Wisdom is supernatural—it isn't taught by men, it is a gift from God.

It is amazing how many people seem to think
that common sense is incompatible with being "spiritual." Spiritual people don't float around all day on
clouds of glory, seeing angels and hearing disem-
bodied voices. You live in a real world with real issues and need real answers. You do the seeking and
He does the speaking, but He is the Spirit of Wisdom and will not tell you to do things that are unwise. If you need real answers in your life, wisdom
and common sense are yours for the asking.

Get Off the Treadmill

But to one who, not working [by the Law], trusts (believes fully) in Him Who justifies the ungodly, his faith is credited to him as righteousness (the standing acceptable to God). Thus David congratulates the man and pronounces a blessing on him to whom God credits righteousness apart from the works he does.

ROMANS 4:5-6

If you spend years on the performance treadmill of the world, it is hard to get off. When you are addicted to feeling good about yourself only when you perform well, you are in for a life of misery. It is a cycle of trying and failing, trying harder and failing again, and feeling guilty and rejected.

God does not want you on the performance treadmill. He wants you to feel good about yourself whether you perform perfectly or not. He doesn't want you to be filled with pride, but He certainly did not create you to reject yourself. If you are trapped on the performance treadmill, ask God to break the cycle in your life. Let your confidence be based on who you are in Christ.

Spirit, Mind, and Body

*And may the God of peace Himself sanctify you
through and through [separate you from profane
things, make you pure and wholly consecrated to
God]; and may your spirit and soul and body be
preserved sound and complete [and found] blameless
at the coming of our Lord Jesus Christ (the Messiah).*

I THESSALONIANS 5:23

Many people do not understand they are a tri-part being: a spirit, soul, and body. You are a spirit, you have a soul, and you live in a body. God promises to take care of all three parts that make you who you are.

You are to work with the Holy Spirit to carry out the plan that began to operate in you when you accepted Jesus as your Lord and Savior. Your new birth begins in your spirit, is carried out through your soul (mind, will, and emotions), and is finally visible to other people through a demonstration of His glory in your physical life. God is working in you as long as you believe. He has begun a good work and He will also finish it.

You Are Not Alone

Because he has set his love upon Me, therefore
will I deliver him; I will set him on high, because
he . . . [has a personal knowledge of My mercy,
love, and kindness—trusts and relies on Me,
knowing I will never forsake him].

PSALM 91:14

God wants you to know you are not alone. Satan wants you to believe you are all alone, but you are not. He wants you to believe no one understands how you feel, but that is not true.

In addition to God being with you, many believers know how you feel and understand what you are experiencing mentally and emotionally.

As God's child, you can claim His wonderful promises. No matter what you are facing or how lonely you may feel, know that you are not alone.

As you meditate on God tonight, draw strength and encouragement from knowing He is always faithful and He will never forsake you.

Lift Up Your Eyes

But You, O Lord, are a shield for me,
my glory, and the lifter of my head.

PSALM 3:3

When you feel down, everything around you seems to fall apart, and you begin to lose your strength. Your head and hands and heart begin to droop. Even your eyes and your voice are lowered.

You are downcast because you are looking at your problems, and this only makes you feel worse. Sometimes you are tempted to say, "Oh, what's the use?" and just give up. But God is waiting for you to lift up your eyes and look to Him for help.

Life will always bring discouraging situations, but you don't have to let them get you down. Despite life's distressing circumstances, you can be confident in the Lord, the lifter of your head.

Lift up your eyes, hands, head, and heart and look not at your problems, but at the one who has promised to see you through to victory. Smile . . . it will lift your spirit.

Expect a Turnaround

As for you, you thought evil against me, but God meant it for good, to bring about that many people should be kept alive, as they are this day.

GENESIS 50:20

This verse is part of the story of how God promoted Joseph to a place of power after his brothers had sold him into slavery. It is a great testament to God's desire and ability to overcome evil with good.

Joseph's brothers meant to destroy him, but Joseph became second in command to Pharaoh and was used by God to save not only his own family but many thousands of others.

Sometimes you forget how big your God is. Whatever may have happened to you in the past, you must understand it doesn't have to dictate your future. Set your faith and trust in God and watch to see how He will turn it around for your good. Rejoice! God has a good plan for your life.

Love by Giving

But if anyone has this world's goods . . . and sees his brother . . . in need, yet closes his heart of compassion against him, how can the love of God live and remain in him? . . . Let us not love [merely] in theory or in speech but in deed and in truth.

1 JOHN 3:17-18

Many people love things and use people to get them. But God intends for you to love people and use things to bless them. Sharing your possessions with others is one way to move love from the "talking about it stage" to the "doing it stage."

God has given you a heart of compassion, but you choose whether to open or close it. There are hurting people all around you, and simple acts of kindness can make these individuals feel loved and valuable.

Don't just strive to have more prosperity; strive to excel in giving. If you do, you will discover God makes sure you have enough to meet your own needs, with plenty to give away.

Live One Day at a Time

*So do not worry or be anxious about tomorrow, for
tomorrow will have worries and anxieties of its own.
Sufficient for each day is its own trouble.*

MATTHEW 6:34

Most of us have enough to handle today
without worrying about tomorrow. God
will give you grace for today, but He will not give
you grace for tomorrow until tomorrow arrives.

So often people worry about something that
never happens. When you begin to think about the
"what ifs," the door opens for fear and worry. Some
people worry so much that their worries become
fear, and often the things people fear manifest in
their life.

Do not allow yourself to dread tomorrow. Just
know that God is faithful. It is comforting to know
that whatever tomorrow may hold, He holds tomorrow. His grace is sufficient to meet the need. Do not
waste today's grace by worrying about tomorrow.
Live one day at a time and you'll be amazed at how
much you can accomplish for Christ.

Change Your Focus

*I pray: that your love may abound yet more and
more and extend to its fullest development . . . so
that you may surely learn to sense what is vital, and
approve and prize what is excellent and of real value.*

PHILIPPIANS 1:9-10

Paul prayed this prayer for the believers at the church in Philippi, knowing they could not have powerful, victorious lives unless they learned the real value of loving others.

You too must make a true commitment to walk in love, which may require you to readjust your priorities and change your focus.

You should have your mind renewed to what love really is. It is not a feeling you have; it is a decision you make—a decision to treat people the way Jesus would treat them.

A true love walk does not come easily or without personal sacrifice, but the benefits are great. God will enrich your life like never before. Loving others is the pathway to true joy.

Let God Increase Your Strength

*He gives power to the faint and weary, and to
him who has no might He increases strength
[causing it to multiply and making it to abound].*

ISAIAH 40:29

When I feel myself starting to get weary,
I go to the Lord. I have learned it's better to keep up regular maintenance than to wait until a breakdown occurs and then try to repair the
damage.

It is wise not to use up everything you have and
totally deplete all your resources—physically, mentally, emotionally, and spiritually.

It's easy to get burned out from overwork or just
being continually upset and frustrated about problems, especially when you focus on them rather than
keeping your eyes on the Lord.

Don't rely on yourself and your own strength
and abilities. God has promised to provide the
strength, energy, and power you need to keep going.
So learn to relax more and allow the Lord to restore
and renew you before you start falling apart. Come
apart daily and spend quality time with Jesus.

Trust God's Timing

I trusted in, relied on, and was confident in
You, O Lord; I said, You are my God. My
times are in Your hands.

PSALM 31:14-15

Trust requires you to place your time in God's hands, believing that His timing is perfect for all things in your life.

Your human nature wants good things to happen in your life now—not later. But as you mature in the Christian life you learn to believe for things not now, but in God's perfect timing.

Trusting God often means not knowing how God is going to accomplish something and not knowing when He will do it. But not knowing "how and when" stretches your faith and teaches you lessons in trust. Remember: Trust is not inherited; it is learned.

Timing plays an important part in learning to trust God. As you experience His faithfulness over and over, you will give up trusting yourself and place your life in His very capable hands. What a wonderful place to be!

Remember God and Take Action

O my God, my life is cast down upon me
[and I find the burden more than I can bear];
therefore will I [earnestly] remember You.

PSALM 42:6

When you are down, the devil wants you to remember every foul, rotten, stinking thing that has ever happened to you and every shameful, detestable, despicable thing you have ever done.

God wants you to remember Him and sing praises to Him in the midst of your miserable situation. Remember you are a new creature; old things have passed away.

When King Saul was assaulted by an evil spirit, he took action. Saul called for David to come play his harp to soothe His troubled spirit (see 1 Samuel 16).

Whenever you feel your spirit starting to sink, you need to take action immediately. Don't wait.

Remember the Lord and the good things He has done for you—it will boost your faith and lift your spirit! Lift your hands in praise and your voice in song. Satan cannot defeat a worshipper.

Don't Exceed Reasonable Limits

Do you not know that your body is the temple . . .
of the Holy Spirit Who lives within you . . .
You are not your own, you were bought with a
price . . . So then, honor God and bring
glory to Him in your body.

1 CORINTHIANS 6:19-20

In today's world, stress is a normal part of everyday life. God created you to withstand normal amounts of pressure and tension, and if you keep stress within reasonable limits, there is no problem. But if you don't, the trouble begins.

Many stressful situations are unavoidable, but too often you cause yourself extra stress by working too hard and too long, not eating and sleeping properly, and getting so involved in activities—even good works—that you exceed wise limits. If you keep adding to that mental and emotional stress, you get into trouble.

If you are pushing yourself beyond reasonable limits, it's time to remember that the Holy Spirit lives in you. You owe it to Him and to yourself to let Him help you recognize and stay within your limits. Don't burn out. Burn on!

Enjoy the Righteousness of Christ

[Righteousness, standing acceptable to God] will be granted and credited to us also who believe in (trust in, adhere to, and rely on) God, Who raised Jesus our Lord from the dead.

ROMANS 4:24

It is an awe-inspiring thing to realize you are in right standing with God simply because you believe in Him. Because Jesus who knew no sin became sin, you are the righteousness of God. What a thrilling and humbling thought.

But the devil doesn't want you to walk in the wonderful thrill of that reality. He wants to bring up all your faults and distract you from the joy of righteousness Jesus died to give you.

Don't let the devil steal the thrill of your righteousness through Christ. As you prepare for a night of rest, spend a few quiet moments thinking about that matchless gift, and worship the one who made it all possible. Go to sleep thinking, "I am the righteousness of God in Christ" (2 Corinthians 5:21).

Heed the Signposts

And your ears will hear a word behind you, say-ing, This is the way; walk in it, when you turn to the right hand and when you turn to the left.

ISAIAH 30:21

Suppose you are driving along the road. In the middle of the road are lines. Some are yellow double lines warning that if you cross them, you run a high risk of being in a head-on col-lision. Some are broken white lines that mean you can cross into the other lane and pass the car in front of you as long as you are cautious and check for on-coming traffic.

There are also signposts that give specific direction or warning: "Detour," "One Way," "Under Construc-tion," "Curve Ahead." If you heed the instructions, you will avoid getting into an unsafe situation.

The same is true in life. There are spiritual sign-posts that instruct us about how to stay under God's protection. If you will heed these signposts, you will be able to safely remain on course. For example, al-ways follow peace and you will be going in the right direction.

Love Man . . . Trust God

Many believed in His name . . . but Jesus
[for His part] did not trust Himself to them . . .
for He Himself knew what was in human nature.
[He could read men's hearts.]

JOHN 2:23-25

Jesus loved people, especially His disciples. He had great fellowship with them, traveled with them, ate with them, and taught them. But He didn't put His trust in them, because He knew human nature.

This doesn't mean He had no trust in His relationship with them; He just didn't open Himself to them in the same way that He trusted in and opened up to His heavenly Father. That is the way you should be.

Many times people form close relationships and depend on their friends to be there for them instead of looking to God. But you don't want to do that. Even in the best relationships, people will disappoint you because people are not perfect.

It is right to love and respect others, but always remember that only God can be counted on to never fail you!

Don't React—Stay Calm

As for you, be calm and cool and steady.

2 TIMOTHY 4:5

If you struggle because of all the trouble in the world and in your life, and you get upset with people who are hard to deal with—here is the solution: Be calm and cool and steady.

When trouble starts in our lives, too often we tend to get upset, saying, "What can I do? What can I do? What can I do?" We immediately react in the flesh instead of seeking the Lord for direction.

This seems to be the way of the world, and if we are not careful, we do what everyone else does. But God has a better plan for His children. Getting all upset and reacting emotionally doesn't help matters—it only causes more problems.

So when trouble rushes in and interrupts your plans, be obedient to God—ask Him to help you be calm, cool, and steady.

Give Until It Hurts

*[They gave] according to their ability, yes, and
beyond their ability; and [they did it] voluntarily.*

2 CORINTHIANS 8:3

There are various levels of giving, and some are less painful than others. One way to be a giver is to use your material possessions to be a blessing. Giving away things you no longer want or use is good, but you should also give away new things, or things that have value to you.

If you know someone who has been through a difficult time, go shopping for that person. Look for that special gift that seems just right. It will take time, and for busy people that is painful, but it is good to stretch yourself in new areas.

Sometimes you may need to give away one of your favorite possessions—and that can be painful. But it is good to get out of your comfort zone and give until it hurts. Jesus gave His all on the cross for your sins. Surely we can endure giving up mere worldly possessions.

Love Not the World

> *Do not love or cherish the world or the things*
> *that are in the world. If anyone loves the world,*
> *love for the Father is not in him.*
>
> 1 JOHN 2:15

Many today are far too attached to the things of this world. Our society is filled to the brim with commerce—there are stores on almost every corner. And everyone is busy making money so they can buy more things. God wants His children to be blessed with nice things, but the Bible tells us not to love them excessively. It is important to keep things in their proper place.

If you use what you have to bless others, God will see to it that you have everything you need, and more. So your goal should be to enjoy the things God gives you and to share with others. This shows your love for the Father.

Trust God and Don't be Afraid

Fear not; stand still (firm, confident, undismayed)
and see the salvation of the Lord which
He will work for you today.

EXODUS 14:13

All of us face times when we feel fear about doing a particular thing. Perhaps the Lord has prompted you to step out and do something, and the devil is trying to keep you from doing it. This verse provides a clear and simple solution: Fear not, don't run, and God will help you.

When you are faced with fear, rather than bowing your knee to it you must stand firm, knowing that God will help you.

Even if your knees are shaking, your mouth is dry, and you feel as though you are getting weak, just keep saying, "Lord, strengthen me. This is what You have told me to do, and with Your help I am going to do it because it is Your revealed will for me. I am determined that my life is not going to be ruled by fear but by Your Word."

Pursue and Seek Love

Eagerly pursue and seek to acquire [this] love
[make it your aim, your great quest].

1 CORINTHIANS 14:1

Developing a love walk like the one displayed in the life of Jesus is like digging for gold. True Christlike love is not found on the surface of life. The Bible says you must eagerly pursue and seek it. This means you must go after love with all your might, as if you cannot live without it.

You must learn all you can about love and familiarize yourself with everything Jesus and the apostles said about it. However, not only are you to learn about love, you are to walk in love, remembering to treat others the way you desire to be treated.

Tonight, ask God to help you seek and acquire His kind of love—the love that can make a meaningful difference in your life . . . and in the lives of those around you.

Trust God's Ways

For my thoughts are not your thoughts, neither are
your ways my ways . . . For as the heavens are higher
than the earth, so are My ways higher than your ways
and My thoughts than your thoughts.

ISAIAH 55:8-9

Did you know a lack of understanding of how God does things can wear you out? If you don't understand His ways, you could end up fighting and resisting things, thinking they are an attack from the devil, when in reality they are an attempt by the Lord to work something good in your life.

You know God does not do bad things. But sometimes you may fail to realize that everything that feels bad *to* you is not necessarily bad *for* you. Reminding yourself that His ways are not your ways will help you trust Him even when your circumstances are hard to understand.

As this busy day comes to a close, just put yourself in the hands of almighty God . . . and rest in the knowledge that He is good and knows what's best.

Stop Worrying

Stop being perpetually uneasy (anxious and wor-
ried) about your life . . . who of you by worrying and
being anxious can add one unit of measure (cubit) to
his stature or to the span of his life?

MATTHEW 6:25,27

Many people worry about everything, including what they will or will not eat or
wear, or what they will do if a particular situation
occurs.

Most of us have enough clothes, adequate food,
comfortable houses, and serviceable cars. But when
things get tough and you are faced with situations
that seem impossible, the devil says, "What are you
going to do now?" The temptation comes to worry
but that isn't the answer.

God wants you to know that worrying doesn't
add to your life—in fact, it will surely shorten it if
you make it a habit.

Your heavenly Father knows about all the things
you need before you ask Him. So stop worrying and
focus your attention on the one who is able to provide everything you need, and more.

Live a Balanced Life

So then, whether you eat or drink, or whatever you
may do, do all for the honor and glory of God.

1 CORINTHIANS 10:31

As a Christian, you must balance your spiritual life with your earthly responsibilities. Some people have a "religious spirit" that causes them to either ignore their earthly tasks or to do them without joy. These people only feel approved by God when they are doing what they think are "spiritual" things.

God wants you to learn that you can communicate with and enjoy Him while doing any number of earthly chores. He wants you to know you can talk with Him throughout the day as well as on bended knee. He is ever-present and always available to fellowship with you and to help with your needs.

It is good to set aside special times to spend with God in prayer and study, but you can also enjoy Him while you're doing other things. This way, you can enjoy life and God at all times, not just during "spiritual times."

Watch and Pray

Keep awake (give strict attention, be cautious and active) and watch and pray, that you may not come into temptation. The spirit indeed is willing, but the flesh is weak.

MATTHEW 26:41

Suppose you knew your house was surrounded by enemy agents and at any moment they might break through the door and attack you. Do you think you would be inclined to stay awake and watch the door?

What would you do if for some reason you couldn't stay awake and watch? Wouldn't you make sure someone else in the family was awake and alerted to the danger?

You need to be just as careful to guard against any potential attacks from the enemy of your soul. The devil is out to get you, and you must watch and pray at all times, asking God to help you when you feel weak.

Ask God to provide the strength you need to overcome any temptation the devil brings your way. Guard your heart and take every thought captive.

Let Go of the Ashes

The Lord has anointed . . . me . . . to grant
[consolation and joy] to those who mourn . . . to give
them an ornament (a garland or diadem) of beauty
instead of ashes, the oil of joy instead of mourning.

ISAIAH 61:1,3

This passage specifically says God wants to give consolation and joy—beauty instead of ashes—for those who mourn. But in order for Him to do that you must let go of the ashes of your past.

Some people have their loved ones cremated and keep their ashes in a box or urn. Eventually they may carry the ashes to a meaningful spot and throw them to the wind. It's a way of letting them go—permanently.

That is what God wants you to do if you have been hurt in the past and are hanging on to the ashes. If you want real joy, let go of those ashes, allowing the wind of the Holy Spirit to blow them out of your life . . . permanently!

Wear God's Armor and Stand Your Ground

Therefore put on God's complete armor, that you may be able to resist and stand your ground on the evil day [of danger], and, having done all [the crisis demands], to stand [firmly in your place].

EPHESIANS 6:13

When the devil comes against you, you must have on the complete armor of God if you are to resist the devil and do all God wants you to do.

You must realize that what you do to overcome one crisis may not be the best way to handle the next crisis. The solution to your problem is not in a certain method or procedure, but in the power God gives you to accomplish what He directs you to do.

When you deal with a crisis, the key is not in your method but in unleashing the power of God through faith. So wear God's armor, stand your ground against the devil, lift up the shield of faith, and see how God will bring the victory!

Be a Blessing Everywhere You Go

He [the benevolent person] scatters abroad;
He gives to the poor; His deeds of justice and
goodness and kindness and benevolence will
go on and endure forever!

2 CORINTHIANS 9:9

It is both good and scriptural to give to the poor—they should be one of your primary concerns. Look for people who are needy and bless them. Share what you have with those who are less fortunate.

But it is also good to remember that *everyone* needs blessings—even the rich, the successful, and those who appear to have everything. What you buy or do for these people is not the real issue; they may not need the gift, but they need the love.

We all get weary sometimes and need to be encouraged, edified, complimented, and appreciated. This can be done with words alone, but it is a nice gesture to add a gift when appropriate.

Remember, God blesses you so you can be a blessing—not only in a few places but everywhere you go!

Discipline Your Thoughts and Words

A man's [moral] self shall be filled with the fruit
of his mouth; and with the consequence of his words
he must be satisfied [whether good or evil]. Death
and life are in the power of the tongue.

PROVERBS 18:20-21

Troubles are a part of life, but God has provided a powerful way for you to free yourself of the worry and anxiety that normally accompany your problems.

God wants good things for your life, but you must cooperate with Him by carefully choosing what you think and speak. By speaking negative words you are inviting negative experiences, but when you speak positive, faith-filled words, you can expect to receive the goodness of God.

Yes, times of trouble are inevitable, but it is during these times that you have the opportunity to discipline your thoughts and words, obey God, and exercise and stretch your faith. When you choose discipline, you are choosing life!

Stop Trying and Start Trusting

[Not in your own strength] for it is God Who is all the while effectually at work in you [energizing and creating in you the power and desire], both to will and to work for His good pleasure and satisfaction and delight.

PHILIPPIANS 2:13

Most of us desire the good life God has planned for us, but we recognize areas in our lives that need to be changed. Many times you set out to make those changes, yet in spite of your best efforts, you seem powerless to make it happen.

Trying to bring about change through your own strength and plans will always result in frustration. God is waiting for you to stop trying to change and start trusting Him to change you.

If you need to make changes in your thoughts, attitudes, and behavior, understand that you can't do it by yourself. Spend time with God and ask for His help—after all, if He can't do it, it can't be done. But He can . . . and He will!

Don't Waste Your Pain

All things work together and are [fitting into a plan] for good to and for those who love God and are called according to [His] design and purpose.

ROMANS 8:28

Life is full of unjust situations that can create a great deal of pain for you, especially in your relationship with other people. You will experience some hurt and pain, but you don't have to allow these experiences to destroy your happiness. You can't always choose what happens to you, but you can choose how you respond to it.

If you've been hurt, God can take your bad experiences and make them work for your good. Believing this truth is a positive decision that can help stop your pain.

Choose to learn from the hurtful experiences instead of wasting your pain by allowing them to make you bitter. One way to do this is to overcome evil with good by making sure you don't hurt others. It's a good place to start!

Hurt . . . Heal . . . Help!

God's love has been poured out in our hearts
through the Holy Spirit Who has been given to us.

ROMANS 5:5

Sometimes people say or do things that hurt you, but you have the God-given ability to love these people. One good way to start is by following the well-known golden rule. It isn't easy. In fact, it requires discipline. But God will help you if you really want to do it.

Discipline is your friend—it is the ability God gives you to walk in His ways. Although it is difficult, discipline is temporary discomfort that can lead to permanent or long-term enjoyment.

If you've been hurt and learned to overcome it, you have a valuable tool to help others. God comforts us so we can comfort others. Here's the progression: We are hurt . . . we allow God to heal us . . . and we are ready to help others. Hurt . . . heal . . . help! It's a process that can literally change your life . . . and the lives of many others around you.

Use the Word as a Weapon

No weapon that is formed against you shall prosper, and every tongue that shall rise against you in judgment you shall show to be in the wrong.

ISAIAH 54:17

Do certain situations in your life always seem to trigger thoughts you don't want and can't seem to get rid of? This is a stronghold the devil has built in your mind—a fortress that attracts and holds a certain kind of thinking. There is a battle going on, and it is taking place in your mind.

God has a great plan for your life, but if you allow yourself to be deceived by the enemy, your wrong thoughts can stop that plan. If you will attack those thoughts with the Word, using it as a weapon against the devil, God will set you free from the strongholds in your mind. He will change your thoughts—and your life—and you will start experiencing that abundance He had planned for you all along.

Let God Have Control

Aim at and seek the [rich, eternal treasures] that
are above . . . And set your minds and keep them set
on what is above . . . not on the things that are on
the earth . . . kill (deaden, deprive of power) the evil
desire . . . [and all that is earthly in you.]

COLOSSIANS 3:1,2,5

It is a natural desire to want to be in control of your life; however, it is not an at-
tainable goal. Assuming you can control all the
people and situations that come into your life is an
unrealistic expectation—and one that leaves you
frustrated, angry, and exhausted.

God has a good plan for everyone that includes a
life far superior to anything the world has to offer,
but attaining it involves dying to self. God relentlessly pursues the flesh—our human nature—and is
intent on setting us free from its control. The
process of letting go and giving up control can be
painful, but the end result is worth it. So let go of
control and let God be God in your life.

Meditate on Him

I will meditate on Your precepts and have respect to Your ways [the paths of life marked out by Your law].

PSALM 119:15

The psalmist said that he thought about or meditated on the precepts of God. In other words, he spent a lot of time pondering and thinking on the ways of God, His instructions, and His teachings. The person who does this, according to Psalm 1:3, is "like a tree firmly planted [and tended] by the streams of water, ready to bring forth its fruit in its season; its leaf also shall not fade or wither; and everything he does shall prosper [and come to maturity]."

The more time you spend meditating on God's Word, the more you will reap from it. The more Word you read and hear, the more power and ability you will have. You will get as much from the Word of God as the effort you put into it. Spend time tonight meditating on God's ways. Choose a Scripture that ministers to you and go to sleep rolling it over and over in your mind.

A Child's Heart

Truly I say to you, unless you repent (change, turn about) and become like little children [trusting, lowly, loving, forgiving], you can never enter the kingdom of heaven [at all]. Whoever will humble himself therefore and become like this little child [trusting, lowly, loving, forgiving] is greatest in the kingdom of heaven.

MATTHEW 18:3-4

Children believe what they are told. Some people say children are gullible, meaning they believe anything no matter how ridiculous it sounds. But children are not gullible—they are trusting. It is a child's nature to trust unless he has experienced something that teaches him otherwise. Your heavenly Father wants you to know that you are His precious little one—His child—and that when you come to Him as such, you show faith in Him, which releases Him to care for you.

God is not like people. If people in your past have hurt you, don't let it affect your relationship with the Lord. You can trust Him. He will care for you as a loving Father.

Don't Dread

Be strong and of good courage. Dread not and
fear not; be not dismayed.

1 CHRONICLES 22:13

Dread is like fear—it draws disaster. It is Satan's open door to bring in the thing feared or dreaded. In Deuteronomy 1:29-30, we read the words of Moses spoken to the children of Israel about their enemies dwelling in the promised land: "Then I said to you, Dread not, neither be afraid of them. The Lord your God Who goes before you, He will fight for you just as He did for you in Egypt before your eyes."

God has not given you a spirit of fear (see 2 Timothy 1:7), and since He did not give you fear, you know He did not give you dread either. Jesus is your Pioneer (see Hebrews 2:10); He goes out ahead of you and makes a way for you. When something seems impossible or unpleasant, trust your Pioneer to go before you and pave the way. Refuse to live in dread and fear.

OK and on Your Way

And I am convinced and sure of this very thing, that He Who began a good work in you will continue until the day of Jesus Christ [right up to the time of His return], developing [that good work] and perfecting and bringing it to full completion in you.

PHILIPPIANS 1:6

None of us has arrived. We are all in the process of becoming. In Romans 7, Paul said the good things he wanted to do, he could not do; and the evil things he did not want to do, he always found himself doing. He said he felt wretched. You can probably relate to that feeling. We all have a long way to go, and Satan seems to enjoy reminding us daily.

If you struggle with a constant sense of failure, adopt a new attitude. Tell yourself tonight, "I am not where I need to be, but thank God I am not where I used to be. I'm okay, and I'm on my way!"

A Reining Ear

*But I say, walk and live [habitually] in the
[Holy] Spirit [responsive to and controlled and
guided by the Spirit]; then you will certainly not
gratify the cravings and desires of the flesh.*

GALATIANS 5:16

Some horses have what their trainers call a "reining ear." While most horses are guided by a bit in their mouths, a few are directed by verbal command. One ear is sensitive to natural warnings; the other is attuned to the voice of the master.

God teaches you what is right, and every single day you must choose. In order to follow God the flesh must be told "no," and the flesh suffers when that happens. You must also understand there may be times when you are galloping full speed ahead in one direction and the Master will tell you to stop and go another way. Like the horse with the "reining ear," you must be willing to follow the Lord in all His leadings. You must learn to say no to self, and yes to God.

The Fruit of the Spirit

But the fruit of the [Holy] Spirit [the work which
His presence within accomplishes] is love, joy
(gladness), peace, patience (an even temper,
forbearance), kindness, goodness (benevolence),
faithfulness, gentleness (meekness, humility),
self-control (self-restraint, continence).

GALATIANS 5:22-23

When the Holy Spirit lives inside you, you have everything He has. His fruit is in you. The seed has been planted. God gives each one of us various gifts to use, but in order to use your gifts in the most powerful way as He desires, you must first allow the fruit to grow up and mature within you by cultivating it. Each time you choose to operate in the fruit of the Spirit it grows.

When you know what God has available for you and you release your faith to walk in it, His Spirit will give you the power you need to produce good fruit. If you are willing to develop the character qualities of God in your life, which is the fruit of the Spirit, you will live an exceptional type of life that is reserved only for His sons and daughters.

Raised from the Dead

Martha then said to Jesus, Master, if You had been here, my brother would not have died.

JOHN 11:21

John 11 records the illness and death of Lazarus, a close friend of Jesus. By the time Jesus arrived Lazarus had already been dead for four days. Like Martha, Mary also told the Lord, "If You had been here, my brother would not have died" (John 11:32).

We all feel like that sometimes. We feel that if Jesus had only shown up sooner maybe things would not be so bad. Verses 23 and 25 tell us how Jesus responded to these words of hopelessness and despair: "Your brother shall rise again. . . . I am [Myself] the Resurrection and the Life. Whoever believes in (adheres to, trusts in, and relies on) Me, although he may die, yet he shall live."

As He promised, Jesus called Lazarus to come forth from the tomb and he did so, totally restored. If Jesus can raise a dead man, surely He can raise a dead circumstance.

Just Do It!

*Do all things without grumbling and faultfinding
and complaining [against God] and questioning and
doubting [among yourselves].*

PHILIPPIANS 2:14

When your feelings get off track, you need to keep them from running your life. You need to submit your will to what God tells you to do through His Word to you. If you don't feel like going to church, go anyway. If you don't feel like giving that special offering God told you to give, do it anyway. If God tells you to give away items you feel like keeping, give them away with joy.

If you really want to be happy and you want God's anointing on your life, you must be obedient to the voice of God—regardless of what you think about it or how you feel. We don't always have to know why God wants us to do something. We just need to know what He tells us to do—and then do it!

From the Inside Out

Bring forth fruit that is consistent with repentance
[let your lives prove your change of heart].

MATTHEW 3:8

Our society places so much importance on the way things look that appearances often take priority over true quality. One time I saw some big, perfect oranges in the grocery store and decided to buy one. I was sure the orange would taste as good as it looked, but when I peeled that beautiful thing and took a bite, it was dry and bitter.

Giving consideration to whether you are as good on the inside as you look on the outside is a serious matter. Many people are searching for God today, and there are numerous teachings about how to find Him that sound right. As Christians, we need to make sure we are "the real thing" and not a phony. Only then will people see Jesus in us and want what we have.

Light and Life

> *In the beginning God (prepared, formed, fashioned, and) created the heavens and the earth. The earth was without form and an empty waste, and darkness was upon the face of the very great deep. The Spirit of God was moving (hovering, brooding) over the face of the waters. And God said, Let there be light; and there was light. And God saw that the light was good (suitable, pleasant) and He approved it; and God separated the light from the darkness.*
>
> GENESIS 1:1-4

You see a spiritual principle at work in these verses—light overpowering darkness. Life overpowering death works the same way. Pour in light and darkness has to flee. Pour in life and death has to flee.

Some people fight with the devil all the time, and while they are doing so they are also speaking death to themselves and their situation. Not only can you overcome death and darkness in your own life by speaking the Word, you can be an effective intercessor in the lives of others.

A Hearing Heart

*So give Your servant an understanding mind
and a hearing heart to judge Your people, that I
may discern between good and bad.*

1 KINGS 3:9

Jesus said, "Take heed that no man deceive you" (Matthew 24:4 KJV). The Bible tells you that in the last days deception will become so rampant that even God's select people could be deceived. There will be people who say they are the Christ, the Messiah, and false prophets who will deceive and lead many people astray. They will even show great signs and wonders. It will be pretty confusing to tell who is who and what is what.

You need a great deal of discernment, and the Bible says you can have it if you seek it. God wants you to ask Him for wisdom, knowledge, and understanding. He wants to give you discretion and discernment. Seek God tonight and ask Him for these things. He will surely bless you with a heart that hears clearly and discerns what is right.

Hang Tough!

And let us not lose heart and grow weary and faint in acting nobly and doing right, for in due time and at the appointed season we shall reap, if we do not loosen and relax our courage and faint.

GALATIANS 6:9

Think about Jesus. Immediately after being baptized and filled with the Holy Ghost, He was led into the wilderness to be tested and tried by the devil. He did not complain and become discouraged and depressed. He did not think or speak negatively. He went through each test victoriously.

Can you imagine Jesus traveling around the country with His disciples talking about how hard everything was? Can you picture Him complaining about how difficult going to the cross was going to be . . . or how uncomfortable it was to roam the countryside with no bed to sleep in at night? You and I have the mind of Christ, and we can handle things the way He did: by being mentally prepared through "victory thinking."

Well-Aimed Stones

And the Word (Christ) became flesh (human,
incarnate) and tabernacled (fixed His tent
of flesh, lived awhile) among us.

JOHN 1:14

Jesus is the Word made flesh who came to dwell among men. Scripture also refers to Jesus as "the Rock," or a stone, as in Luke 20:17, where He is called the chief Cornerstone. If Jesus is the Word made flesh, and if He is the Rock, then each portion of the Word is like a stone.

Instructions were given to the Israelites concerning how to handle their enemy in Deuteronomy 13:10, "And you shall stone him to death with stones, because he has tried to draw you away from the Lord your God." Remember that David defeated Goliath with a well-aimed stone.

You too can "stone" your enemy, Satan, in accordance with Deuteronomy 30:14, "But the word is very near you, in your mouth and in your mind and in your heart." Learn the Word and allow the Holy Spirit to teach you how to speak it effectively.

Fiery Trials

Rejoice and exult in hope; be steadfast and patient in suffering and tribulation; be constant in prayer.

ROMANS 12:12

I've heard *patience* defined as "a fruit of the Spirit that can only be developed under trial." Really, you cannot develop patience any other way. That means the only way you can develop the fruit of patience is by being around obnoxious people who drive you crazy; waiting in backed-up traffic; waiting in endless grocery store lines; waiting for breakthroughs; waiting for your healing; waiting for people in your life to change; and waiting for yourself to change.

Be patient with yourself! Be patient with your own spiritual growth. Be patient with God if He's not coming through at the time you'd like Him to. Be patient with people; be patient with circumstances. Be patient because in patience you possess your soul. James 1:4 says that the patient man is perfect and entire, lacking in nothing.

Above Every Name

*That in (at) the name of Jesus every
knee should (must) bow, in heaven and on
earth and under the earth.*

PHILIPPIANS 2:10

Speaking the name of Jesus and having a revelation about the power in that name are two different things. Releasing the power in the name of Jesus requires a supernatural revelation. When you speak the name of Jesus in faith, His name is so powerful that every knee must bow in three realms—in heaven, on earth, and under the earth!

Think about this tonight: Jesus came from the highest heaven, He has been to the earth, and has descended to Hades, or under the earth, and now is seated at the right hand of the Father once again in the highest heaven. He has filled everything and everywhere with Himself. He is seated above everything else and has a name that is above every other name. His name is the highest name, the most powerful name—and His name has been given to us!

Cast Your Care

Therefore humble yourselves [demote, lower your-
selves in your own estimation] under the mighty hand
of God, that in due time He may exalt you, casting the
whole of your care [all your anxieties, all your worries,
all your concerns, once and for all] on Him, for He cares
for you affectionately and cares about you watchfully.

I PETER 5:6-7

This passage of Scripture tells you to humble yourself and not worry. Worry is the mind racing around trying to find a solution to its situation. A person who worries still thinks that in some way he can solve his own problem. But only God can deliver you and in every situation your first response should be to lean on Him.

When the enemy tries to give you a problem, you have the privilege of casting it upon God. The word *cast* actually means to pitch or throw. You and I can pitch our problems to God and He will catch them. He knows exactly what to do with them.

Loving Correction

For the time being no discipline brings joy, but seems grievous and painful; but afterwards it yields a peaceable fruit of righteousness to those who have been trained by it.

HEBREWS 12:11

When we need correction—and we all need it at one time or another—it is the Lord's desire to correct us Himself. Whom the Lord loves, He chastens (see Hebrews 12:6). God's correction or chastisement is not a bad thing; it is always and ultimately only for your good.

The fact that it works toward your good does not mean it always feels good or that it is something you enjoy immediately. In fact, correction can be one of the most difficult things to receive—especially when it comes through another person. Even if you have problems, you don't want others to know you have them. Usually God prefers to correct you privately, but if you won't accept His correction, He will use whatever tools are at His disposal. In Balaam's case, God used his donkey! Whatever God decides to use to correct us, we should submit to Him knowing that He loves us and only has our ultimate good in mind.

A More Excellent Way

And this I pray: that your love may abound yet
more and more and extend to its fullest development
in knowledge and all keen insight [that your love
may display itself in greater depth of acquaintance
and more comprehensive discernment].

PHILIPPIANS 1:9

When something abounds, it grows and becomes so big that it chases people down, overtaking and overwhelming them. This is how Paul prayed for the church—that love would abound. Then he said, "So that you may surely learn to sense what is vital, and approve and prize what is excellent and of real value" (Philippians 1:10).

It is very important to be a person of excellence—to do your very best every day in all you believe God is asking you to do . . . to do every job to the best of your ability. You can't be an excellent person and not walk in love, and you can't walk in love and not be an excellent person. To abound in love is the most excellent thing you can do.

Sun, Moon, and Stars

The sun is glorious in one way, the moon is glorious in another way, and the stars are glorious in their own [distinctive] way; for one star differs from and surpasses another in its beauty and brilliance.

I CORINTHIANS 15:41

We are all different. Like the sun, moon, and stars, God has created us to be different from one another, and He has done it on purpose. Each of us fills a need, and we are all part of God's overall plan. When you struggle to be like others, not only do you lose yourself, you also grieve the Holy Spirit. God wants you to fit into His plan, not to feel pressured trying to fit into everyone else's plans.

We are all born with different temperaments, different physical features, different fingerprints, different gifts and abilities, etc. Your goal should be to find out what you individually are supposed to be, and then succeed at being that. Different is good!

Declare the Word

I have declared from the beginning the former
things [which happened in times past to Israel];
they went forth from My mouth and I made
them known; then suddenly I did them,
and they came to pass [says the Lord].

ISAIAH 48:3

Notice God's method of operation: first He declares things, and then He does them. God wanted Israel to know that it was He who was doing the great works in their lives, so He announced them ahead of time. This explains why God sent the prophets. They came speaking forth into the earth God-inspired, God-instructed words that brought forth God's will from the spiritual realm into the natural. Even Jesus did not come to the earth until first the prophets had spoken about Him for hundreds of years.

God operates through spiritual laws that He has set in place, and you cannot ignore them. You are created in His image and are expected to follow His example. Declare the Word of the Lord in your life! Speak it, believe it, and watch God bring it to pass.

A Faithful Servant

*So then, let us [apostles] be looked upon as
ministering servants of Christ and stewards
(trustees) of the mysteries (the secret purposes)
of God. Moreover, it is [essentially] required of
stewards that a man should be found faithful
[proving himself worthy of trust].*

I CORINTHIANS 4:1-2

A faithful person knows what God has put in their heart, and even though they may feel like quitting, they don't give up. They don't get out of a relationship because it isn't easy anymore. They don't leave a church because there is some "new" thing across town, or a job because it gets too challenging.

One of the most important lessons you can learn is to be faithful with something until God lets you know you are finished with it. Sometimes God will call you out of one place and put you into another one—but God doesn't change the plan very frequently. A faithful person is committed to doing whatever God tells them to do—no matter what!

Don't Be Caught Sleeping

All of you must keep awake (give strict attention,
be cautious and active) and watch and pray,
that you may not come into temptation. The
spirit indeed is willing, but the flesh is weak.

MATTHEW 26:41

Jesus wanted the disciples to pray with Him, but they kept falling asleep. He was trying to prepare them for the trial that was coming. He was saying, "Don't sleep, pray! You're going to be tempted beyond what you can bear if you don't pray." As Jesus prayed, an angel came and strengthened Him in spirit enabling Him to endure the cross. But the disciples didn't pray—they slept— and proved that the flesh truly is weak.

Your spirit is willing to do what is right, but your flesh will not help you. Your flesh will rule you if you don't pray and ask God to strengthen you in spirit and to help you resist temptation. Your flesh may be tired tonight, but spend some time in prayer. You don't know what tests may come tomorrow.

Take a Stand

Oh, how great is Your goodness, which You have
laid up for those who fear, revere, and worship You,
goodness which You have wrought for those who trust
and take refuge in You before the sons of men!

PSALM 31:19

The phrase, "before the sons of men" means that if you will not be a closet Christian, but live for Jesus openly before others, God will store up His goodness for you.

Many Christians aren't comfortable talking about their faith. We all have moments where we don't take a stand for God like we should. Maybe we are afraid of being rejected, isolated, or ridiculed. It can feel awkward to say, "I really don't want to hear a dirty joke. I'm a Christian and I'm not interested in going to an inappropriate movie, or hitting the bars after work. That's not what I'm about. My relationship with God is too important to me."

You should not be a lukewarm, wishy-washy Christian. When you take an uncompromising stand for Christ, God will reward you openly.

Waiting on His Goodness

I will make all My goodness pass before you. . . .
Behold, there is a place beside Me, and you shall
stand upon the rock, and while My glory passes by, I
will put you in a cleft of the rock and cover you
with My hand until I have passed by. Then I
will take away My hand and you shall see
My back; but My face shall not be seen.

EXODUS 33:19,21-23

In times of trouble God hides you in Christ. Safe in the cleft of the Rock, there is provision for your needs. It may not be everything you want, but He gives you what you need to get through the situation.

Perhaps you are facing difficulty and have been waiting and waiting to see God's glory. God desires to pour out His goodness upon you. He has covered you with His hand and is continually moving toward you with the answer. You may not see Him coming, but you will certainly know when He has been there!

Wise Choices

Look carefully then how you walk! Live purpose-
fully and worthily and accurately, not as the unwise
and witless, but as wise (sensible, intelligent people).

EPHESIANS 5:15

Many times you ask God to speak to you, but if He doesn't respond with a specific word, you still have to live your daily life. You make decisions every day, and He doesn't dictate every little choice you make. When you don't get a *rhema* (spoken word) from God, you need to use wisdom to make good choices. He expects you to handle some issues on your own. You shouldn't always require a "big word" from God.

For example, if you want to buy something and wonder if you should, the first obvious question you need to ask yourself is, "Can I afford it?" If not, then wisdom would say, "Don't buy it!" The audible voice of God is not needed when wisdom is already shouting the truth. You need to be mature enough to do what you already know is right.

The Work of Patience

I waited patiently and expectantly for the Lord;
and He inclined to me and heard my cry.

PSALM 40:1

Any time you become frustrated and start trying to make things happen on your own, it is a sure sign you are not being patient with God. You need to practice waiting on God and let Him do what He wants to do, in His way and time. The best definition of *patience* I have ever heard is "to be constant or to be the same all the time, no matter what is going on." Patience is not merely waiting; it is how you act while you are waiting.

The hardest thing most of us will ever have to do as Christians is wait on the Lord. You will undoubtedly have to wait on many things during your lifetime. Waiting is not optional. But it is during the waiting periods of life that the most powerful things will happen within you.

Enjoy the Journey

Make a joyful noise to the Lord, all you lands!
Serve the Lord with gladness! Come before
His presence with singing!

PSALM 100:1-2

So many Christians are headed somewhere, but not many of us are enjoying
the trip. It would be such a tragedy to arrive at the
end of your journey only to realize you had not en-
joyed life to its fullest. Often, you think you must do
something great, and you forget the simple things
that bless the Lord. Serving the Lord with gladness
is a worthy goal. He rejoices when your heart is
filled with joy and your mouth is filled with praise.

You should be determined to finish your course.
But like Paul, you should strive to run the race with
joy. Whatever your present station in life, whatever
you are called to do, wherever you are called to go,
enjoy the journey. Don't waste one day of the precious life God has given you. Rejoice in the Lord,
and again I say, rejoice!

Love Is Not a Feeling

Little children, let us not love [merely] in
theory or in speech but in deed and in truth
(in practice and in sincerity).

1 JOHN 3:18

This Scripture tells you that love is not simply a theory, a feeling, or sweet nothings whispered in the ear—love is deeds. Many people have the mistaken belief that love is a warm, fuzzy feeling. This is why you think you can't love someone who is unpleasant or even hostile. But the truth is that love is an action, doing what needs to be done in every situation. Developing love isn't a horrible struggle—it is simply being good to people.

Take a few minutes tonight to examine your life and seek God more about your love walk. How kind are you to people? What are you doing for others? How are you treating people who aren't treating you very nicely? Change your direction if you haven't been expressing God's love to others through joy, peace, patience, goodness, and kindness. Don't just talk about love, *walk* in love!

Power from Heaven

But you shall receive power (ability, efficiency, and might) when the Holy Spirit has come upon you, and you shall be My witnesses in Jerusalem and all Judea and Samaria and to the ends (the very bounds) of the earth.

ACTS 1:8

It is possible to fill a glass with water without filling it to full capacity. Likewise when you are born again you have the Holy Spirit in you, but you may not yet be totally filled with the Spirit. Many Christians are very busy doing things for God but don't have enough power in their lives to be what God wants us to be.

Going through the motions and following religious formulas is a waste of time. You must have the revelation that Jesus is alive within you and allow Him to change you and make you a new creature in Christ. Don't tuck God away for emergencies and Sunday mornings. Allow Him to work freely in every area of your life through the power of the Holy Spirit.

A Better Blueprint

We are assured and know that [God being a
partner in their labor] all things work together
and are [fitting into a plan] for good to and
for those who love God and are called according
to [His] design and purpose.

ROMANS 8:28

Notice here that Paul does not say that all things are good, but that all things work together for good. Paul also says in Romans 12:16 to "readily adjust yourself to [people, things]." You must learn to become the kind of person who plans things but who doesn't fall apart if that plan doesn't work out.

Perhaps your car doesn't start tomorrow. You can think, "I knew it! My plans always fail." Or you can tell yourself, "Well, I'll go later when the car is fixed. There is probably some reason I need to be at home today, so I'm going to enjoy my time here." Relax and trust God to work out the details of your life—His blueprint is always best.

Be of Good Cheer

In the world you have tribulation and trials and
distress and frustration; but be of good cheer [take
courage; be confident, certain, undaunted]! For I have
overcome the world. [I have deprived it of power to
harm you and have conquered it for you.]

JOHN 16:33

Life in today's world can be stressful and frustrating—but as a Christian you do not have to operate on the world's system. Yes, you will face difficult and trying situations, but you can refuse to be agitated, disturbed, and upset (see John 14:27).

Even in the midst of your problems you can be happy and confident, cheerful and courageous. Now that's good news!

When you come to the end of a tiring and frustrating day, it is good to spend time with God, thanking Him for overcoming the world on your behalf. Reflecting on His goodness will calm your spirit and prepare you for a peaceful night of rest.

Choose Your Words Carefully

Let no foul or polluting language, nor evil word
nor unwholesome or worthless talk [ever] come out
of your mouth, but only such [speech] as is good
and beneficial to the spiritual progress of others,
as is fitting to the need and the occasion, that
it may be a blessing and give grace (God's
favor) to those who hear it.

EPHESIANS 4:29

As a Christian, you have an awesome responsibility with regard to the words you speak. The Bible tells us that words are containers for power—either creative or destructive. You can tear down or build up the people around you by what you say.

There is an abundance of discouragement coming from the world, but you have the great privilege of bringing encouragement to others by being positive in a negative world.

It can be difficult however, so I encourage you to ask God to help you choose words that will bring positive changes in the lives of others . . . and in your own life too!

Give Yourself a Break

*And I am convinced and sure of this very thing,
that He Who began a good work in you will continue
until the day of Jesus Christ [right up to the time of
His return], developing [that good work] and perfecting and bringing it to full completion in you.*

PHILIPPIANS 1:6

If you find it difficult to like yourself, you are not alone. I struggled with self rejection during much of my life and I have discovered many others also struggle with the same thing. But that is not God's plan. He doesn't want you to feel afraid and insecure . . . or to be consumed with achieving perfection in hopes of being considered valuable.

God is the only one who can perfect the good work He has started in your life, but it takes some time. And during the process He wants you to recognize you are making progress. So give yourself a break and say, "I'm okay and I'm on my way!"

Lighten Up

Anxiety in a man's heart weighs it down,
but an encouraging word makes it glad.

PROVERBS 12:25

If you struggle with anxiety you know about the uneasiness, worry, and feeling of heaviness that come with it. Often it is a general feeling of fear that has no specific cause or source.

Many serious things are going on in the world and you need to be aware of them and prepare for them. But you also need to learn to relax and take things as they come without getting all nervous and upset.

You need to learn how to enjoy the good life God has provided for you through the death and resurrection of His Son Jesus Christ (see John 10:10). So the next time you are tempted to become anxious or upset, think about what you are doing, and find something to be happy about. Have a talk with yourself about all the good things God has done in your life.

Let God Build Your House

Except the Lord builds the house, they labor in vain who build it; except the Lord keeps the city, the watchman wakes but in vain. It is vain for you to rise up early, to take rest late, to eat the bread of [anxious] toil—for He gives [blessings] to His beloved in sleep.

PSALM 127:1-2

As a responsible adult who works hard at doing things right and trying to build a good life for yourself and your family, you may sometimes forget God is the Master Builder.

It is right for you to work and provide the material things you need in life, but only God can build you into all that you should be. This can only happen as you fully yield yourself to Him and allow Him to do the work.

Only the Spirit can cause you to grow into the perfection of Christ . . . He has started a good work in you and He will also finish it, so cooperate with the Master Builder and enjoy the blessings of the beloved . . . even as you sleep.

Believe in God

*For we have heard of your faith in Christ Jesus
[the leaning of your entire human personality on
Him in absolute trust and confidence in His
power, wisdom, and goodness] and of the love
which you [have and show] for all the saints
(God's consecrated ones).*

COLOSSIANS 1:4

Faith is the leaning of the entire human personality on God in absolute trust. That means you need to lean all of yourself on God, believing that only He can accomplish His will and purpose in your life. Your only job is to abide in Him through faith.

John 6:29 says, "This is the work (service) that God asks of you: that you believe in the One Whom He has sent [that you cleave to, trust, rely on, and have faith in His Messenger]."

As you are quiet before the Lord at the end of your day, believe and lean your entire personality on Him in absolute trust and confidence.

Acknowledge God

*In all your ways know, recognize, and
acknowledge Him, and He will direct and
make straight and plain your paths.*

PROVERBS 3:6

Acknowledging the Lord in all your ways
means submitting all your plans to Him
and allowing Him to work them out according to
His will and desire for you. He wants you to come
to know Him in the power of His resurrection (see
Philippians 3:10).

It is a sign of maturity to seek God for who He
is and not only for what He can do for you. So as you
pause at the end of your day, seek God's face (His
presence) and get to know your wonderful, loving
heavenly Father better. Acknowledge His power and
experience the joy of walking in the paths He
chooses for you.

A Time for Everything

*To everything there is a season, and a time for
every matter or purpose under heaven.*

ECCLESIASTES 3:1

If it seems you have been struggling forever with negative things in your life, don't despair. There is a time and season for everything, and bad things ultimately give way to better things.

Even the good things going on in your life may not stay exactly the same, because things are always changing. Sometimes changes are exciting . . . and sometimes they are difficult. But Jesus never changes—and as long as you keep your eyes on Him, you will make it through the changes in your life and continue growing.

Be careful not to get too attached to people, places, positions, or things, but always be free to move with the Spirit. Let go of what lies behind and press on to what lies ahead (see Philippians 3:13-14). Reach toward the new horizon God has for you. You will be glad you did.

Deposit Yourself with God

*Those who are ill-treated and suffer in accordance
with God's will must do right and commit their souls
[in charge as a deposit] to the One Who created
[them] and will never fail [them].*

I PETER 4:19

The same as you deposit money in the
bank, trusting them to take care of it, you
should also deposit yourself with God, trusting Him
to take care of you. As you pray tonight, release
yourself and all that concerns you to God.

If you are spending so much time trying to take
care of yourself and make sure nobody is taking advantage of you that you have no time left to enjoy
your life, it's time to deposit yourself into God's
care. You can trust Him . . . for He never fails.

Offer a Sacrifice of Praise

*Through Him, therefore, let us constantly and at
all times offer up to God a sacrifice of praise, which is
the fruit of lips that thankfully acknowledge and
confess and glorify His name.*

HEBREWS 13:15

The Bible teaches that you must acknowledge and glorify God and offer up a sacrifice of praise regardless of what you may be going through.

Perhaps you have been experiencing a time of trouble in your life, and you have been praying and trusting God to meet the need . . . but nothing has changed. While you are waiting for the answer is a perfect time to offer a sacrifice of praise.

It is easy to praise God when everything is going well, but when you acknowledge and glorify Him in the midst of a troubling situation, that is a sacrifice—and it does not go unnoticed. So offer a sacrifice of praise as you spend time with God at the end of your day.

You Can Pass the Test

Consider it a sheer gift, friends, when tests and
challenges come at you from all sides. You know that
under pressure, your faith-life is forced into the
open and shows its true colors. So don't try to
get out of anything prematurely. Let it do its
work so you become mature and well-
developed, not deficient in any way.

JAMES 1:2-4 THE MESSAGE

When life is filled with tests and trials, you sometimes feel like throwing in the towel. You are tempted to think God doesn't know where you are and what you're going through . . . or that He doesn't care. But God permits tests in your life so He can bless you. And if you are faithful, you will see good results.

If you want to enjoy your Christian life and be used by God to help others, you must maintain a godly attitude during the time of testing. So cooperate with God and display an attitude of faith, and you will pass the test with flying colors!

Practice the Presence of God

*And the Lord said, My Presence shall go
with you, and I will give you rest.*

EXODUS 33:14

This was God's reply to Moses when he asked about the particulars of the mission he had been given and how he could get to know God better. God simply assured Moses that His presence would be with him and give him rest. This was considered by God to be a great privilege. To Him, it was all that Moses needed.

What was true for Moses is true for you. As much as you would like to know God's plans and ways for you, all you really need to know is that His presence will be with you wherever He sends you and in whatever He gives you to do.

So when you get concerned that things aren't going the way you think they should, just remember that God's presence is with you and enjoy the rest He promised to give you.

Learn to Wait with Patience

Do not become sluggish, but imitate those who through faith and patience inherit the promises.

HEBREWS 6:12 NKJV

Experiencing trials while you're waiting to receive something God has promised you can be very difficult. But when you understand how important it is to wait, it makes it worthwhile. This Scripture in Hebrews tells you that you inherit God's promises only through faith and patience.

When you have trials, you grow—or at least you can grow if you learn to develop patience. God does not change, and He says you receive through faith and patience. So you must adapt to His ways—and doing things God's way can bring peace and joy to any situation.

Patience is a fruit of the Spirit . . . and a powerful witness to others. So when you're experiencing a difficult trial, exercise patience. It is like a muscle—the more you use it the stronger it gets.

Be Transformed, Not Conformed

Do not be conformed to this world . . . but be trans-
formed (changed) by the [entire] renewal of your
mind . . . so that you may prove [for yourselves] what
is the good and acceptable and perfect will of God.

ROMANS 12:2

God's will for you is transformation, which takes place from the inside out . . . not conformation, which is someone's external, superficial idea of what you should be; nor your own efforts to conform to their ideas, expectations, and demands.

Often the world wants to draw the borders of a box and put you in it. But this won't work because the box is not God's design.

Most people think you should do what they are doing—that you should be a part of their plan. This is wonderful if God agrees, but when God says no we must say no also.

In this quiet moment determine that you will not be conformed to the wishes of your friends and relatives, but that you will be transformed and led by the Spirit of God.

Live in the Now

But instantly He spoke to them, saying,
Take courage! I AM! Stop being afraid!

MATTHEW 14:27

This was Jesus' response to the disciples when they encountered a storm while out in a boat. He was saying, "I AM here for you right now, and you must have faith now that everything is going to be all right."

That is how you should be living your life—with a "now" faith. Today you can have faith that yesterday and all of its mistakes can be taken care of by God. You can also have faith today that tomorrow will be taken care of when it arrives. But don't waste today worrying about yesterday or tomorrow. Jesus is the great "I Am" and He is here for you today!

God wants you to live for today. Worrying about yesterday or tomorrow steals today. But the great I AM has given you just enough grace for today. Grace for yesterday is all used up and grace for tomorrow will not come until tomorrow. So use the favor and power of the Holy Spirit to do His will right now.

Love with Your Thoughts

For as he thinks in his heart, so is he.

PROVERBS 23:7

You make a mistake when you have the opinion that your thoughts don't affect other people. You can often feel the thoughts of others, and they can feel your thoughts.

Your thoughts not only affect others, they also affect you in a most amazing way. This verse in Proverbs teaches you that you become what you think.

If you think loving thoughts, you become loving. But often you think things about people that you would never say to them, not realizing that even your thoughts can affect them. It is virtually impossible to treat people in a loving way if you are thinking angry thoughts about them.

This is a good lesson for you. It is possible to sin in thought, word, or deed, so if you want to be a loving person you must choose to think good thoughts about other people. Learn to love with your thoughts—it will be good for you and others.

Follow Wisdom

*I, Wisdom [from God], make prudence my
dwelling, and I find out knowledge and discretion.*

PROVERBS 8:12

There is a lot of powerful information in
this small Scripture—information you
would do well to explore. In the Scriptures, being
prudent means being good stewards or managers of
the gifts that God has given you to use. Those gifts
include time, energy, strength, and health, as well as
material possessions.

Each of us has been given a different set of gifts,
and each of us has different abilities to manage those
gifts. It is your individual responsibility to develop
knowledge and discretion as to how you can best use
your gifts. You do this by listening to the Lord and
obeying what He tells you to do.

Following Wisdom is an excellent choice—one
that will bring you many blessings!

Accept and Share the Love of God

We love Him, because He first loved us.

1 JOHN 4:19

More than anything, you need a revelation of God's love for you personally. God's love for you is the foundation for your faith, your freedom from sin, and your ability to step out in ministry to others without fear in the form of insecurity.

God made you with a longing in your heart to be loved. And the Word assures you that God loves you. Yet many people mistakenly believe they have worn God out with their failures. You can't cause God not to love you. Love isn't something God does—it is who He is (see 1 John 4:8).

As you meditate on God's love at the end of the day, accept it and express your great love for Him. Then as you go about your day tomorrow—and all your tomorrows—share that love with others.

Focus on God Instead of Your Fear

Fear not . . . for I am with you; do not look around
you in terror and be dismayed, for I am your
God. I will strengthen and harden you to
difficulties . . . I am the Lord, Who says
to you, Fear not; I will help you!

ISAIAH 41:10,13

Notice this passage tells you not to look around you in terror and be dismayed. When you look at your circumstances until you become afraid it is always a mistake—yet that's just what many people do.

The more you focus your eyes and your mouth on the problem, the more fearful you become. Instead you should focus on God who is able to handle anything you will ever have to face. He has promised to strengthen you and to harden you to difficulties.

No matter how great and important or small and insignificant your fears may be, God is saying to you, "Fear not; I will help you!"

Trust God, Not Yourself

Lean on, trust in, and be confident in the Lord
with all your heart and mind and do not rely
on your own insight or understanding.

PROVERBS 3:5

When you face times of crisis in life you need direction. All of your human reasoning will not provide the answer—it will only add to your confusion. But God will give you direction if you trust Him.

This truth is sometimes difficult for you to deal with because your human nature wants to understand everything. You want things to make sense, but the Holy Spirit can cause you to have peace about things that make no sense at all to your natural mind.

If you are hurting because of a crisis in your life, you must not become angry with God. He is the only one who can help you. Only He can bring the lasting comfort and healing you need. So continue to believe in the goodness of God and lean on, trust in, and be confident in Him.

Give It Up!

Unto You, O Lord, do I bring my life.

PSALM 25:1

This is a very short but powerful verse. In fact it gives you the answer for your whole life: give it to the Lord.

This doesn't mean you should bring Him just your worries and problems. It means bringing Him your entire existence and everything it entails. Grasping that truth will set you free from weariness and a feeling of wanting to give up.

I used to get worn out preparing for my meetings. I would get so intense about it and work so hard at making sure everything was right that I worked myself into exhaustion. Then I learned that all I have to do is give Him my life and everything in it. As we yield to Him, His peace fills us.

As you pray tonight, give your entire life to God and experience the freedom of knowing that whatever you face—good or bad—He has it under control.

Enjoy Everyday Life

Go your way . . . And be not grieved and de-
pressed, for the joy of the Lord is your strength.

NEHEMIAH 8:10

I spent a lot of time in years gone by learning to enjoy my life. The key phrase is *my life*. I learned not to covet someone else's life, but to enjoy mine. It has not been easy and I am still learning. But one thing I do know is that it is God's will for you to enjoy the life He has provided. The joy of the Lord is your strength. You must make a decision to enjoy everyday life.

Enjoying life does not mean you have something exciting going on all the time; it simply means you enjoy simple, everyday things. Most of life is rather ordinary, but you are supernaturally equipped with the power of God to live ordinary everyday life in an extraordinary way.

Live life to the fullest and be a witness to the power of God that is available to everyone.

Keep Looking to Jesus

*Let us run with patient endurance and steady and
active persistence the appointed course of the race
that is set before us, looking away [from all that will
distract] to Jesus. . . . Just think of Him . . . so that
you may not grow weary or exhausted, losing heart
and relaxing and fainting in your minds.*

HEBREWS 12:1-3

It doesn't take any special talent to give
up, lie down on the side of the road of
life, and say, "I quit." Any unbeliever can do that.

But once you get hold of Jesus—or, more accurately, He gets hold of you—He begins to pump
strength, energy, and courage into you, and something strange and wonderful begins to happen. He
won't let you quit!

You may say, "Oh, Lord, I don't want to go on
anymore." But He won't let you give up, even if you
want to. So keep looking to Jesus and follow His example. When you do, you will keep pressing on no
matter what comes your way.

Live in the Liberty of God

Therefore let us not judge one another anymore,
but rather resolve this, not to put a stumbling
block or a cause to fall in our brother's way.

ROMANS 14:13 NKJV

There are many things you cannot do, but there are also numerous things you can do, and do well. You don't have to compare yourself or your abilities and accomplishments with those of others. You are free to follow the God-given plan for your life.

Each of us must have the liberty to be led of God. We even have the right to make our own mistakes and learn from them.

If you allow other people to become a law to you, thinking you must be like them, it steals your freedom, and it's no one's fault but your own. Likewise you must not judge others or expect them to be like you.

Determine now that you will enjoy the liberty of living in God's will . . . and allow others to live in liberty as well.

You Are a New Creation

*Therefore if any person is [ingrafted] in Christ (the
Messiah) he is a new creation (a new creature
altogether); the old [previous moral and
spiritual condition] has passed away.
Behold, the fresh and new has come!*

2 CORINTHIANS 5:17

When you are born again God conse-
crates or dedicates you to a new and different use, the one for which you were intended in
the first place. You get a fresh new opportunity for
service.

When Christ comes to live inside of you, an im-
perishable seed is planted within you. Everything
you need to be completely healthy and whole is in
Him. And if it is in Him, it is in you. But it is in seed
form, and seeds have to be watered and nourished in
order to grow and produce fruit.

You do this by reading and studying the Word of
God and being a doer of the Word. Don't let the
seed lie dormant inside you. Be the fresh new creation God wants you to be.

Rest for Your Soul

*Come to Me, all you who labor and are heavy-
laden and overburdened, and I will cause you to rest.
[I will ease and relieve and refresh your souls.]*

MATTHEW 11:28

Just as you can be involved in outward activity, you can be involved in inward activity. God wants you not only to enter into His rest in your body, but in your soul as well.

To me, finding rest, relief, ease, refreshment, recreation, and blessed quiet for my soul means finding freedom from mental activity. It means not having to constantly try to figure out what I should do about everything in my life . . . trying to come up with answers I don't have. I don't have to worry; instead I can remain in a place of quiet rest.

At the end of a tiring day, you can experience this peace and rest by going to Christ and allowing Him to relieve and refresh your soul. What a wonderful privilege!

Love One Another

*[Let your] love be sincere . . . hate what is evil
[loathe all ungodliness, turn in horror from wicked-
ness], but hold fast to that which is good. Love one
another with brotherly affection, . . . giving prece-
dence and showing honor to one another.*

ROMANS 12:9-10

As a Christian, you are to have sincere
love—God's kind of love. God doesn't
always love the way people act or the things they do,
but He always loves them as people.

God calls you to that same kind of love. You
don't have to like everything someone does—in fact
you are told to turn from wickedness—but it is
your Christian responsibility to follow the example
of Christ. When you recognize that everyone is
God's creation, it is easier to obey His command to
love and honor them.

You must have a loving attitude toward people,
an attitude that is filled with mercy, kindness, and
sincere love. This doesn't always come easy, but God
will provide the strength you need to show His kind
of love to others.

Prepare for Promotion

Dear friends, do not be surprised at the painful trial you are suffering, as though something strange were happening to you. But rejoice that you participate in the sufferings of Christ, so that you may be overjoyed when his glory is revealed.

1 PETER 4:12-13 NIV

Painful trials are a part of life but God loves you and helps you to grow through them. Each challenge you encounter in life is part of your education process—a process that determines when you're ready to be promoted to the next level.

Trials build spiritual muscle, faith, endurance, and longsuffering. They are opportunities to experience firsthand the faithfulness of God and to show your ability to rejoice as you share in the sufferings of Christ.

Trials come and go, but the development of godly character—your personal spiritual maturity—during the process makes you a worthy candidate for the promotion God has planned for you!

Becoming the Righteousness of God

For our sake He made Christ [virtually] to be sin
Who knew no sin, so that in and through Him we
might become . . . the righteousness of God.

2 CORINTHIANS 5:21

This verse gives you cause for great rejoicing, but the enemy tries to undermine your joy by pointing out you don't measure up to God's standard. That's when you must boldly declare that God has done a good work in you and you are in the process of change.

When you accept salvation there is nothing you can do to make God love you any more or less than He already does. This doesn't mean you don't sin anymore or that when you do sin you can just dismiss it. It simply means God loves you even while you are in the process of becoming like Christ. You have not arrived yet, but you are making progress.

God understands that growing and learning is a process, and He wants you to enjoy yourself while you're on the way to reaching the goal.

Sleep in Peace

In peace I will both lie down and sleep, for
You, Lord, alone make me dwell in
safety and confident trust.

PSALM 4:8

In the quiet of the evening after a long day, it's not unusual to think about and evaluate the events of the day. But thoughts can be disturbing, especially if you faced problems that remain unsolved.

Sometimes these thoughts are not easy to turn off and can threaten to rob you of a peaceful night's sleep. But staying awake and worrying will not change or improve the situation at all.

This is a good time to share your concerns with God and ask for His help. He tells us in His Word to cast our cares on Him, so give your thoughts to Him and trust Him to provide a solution. Then lie down and sleep in peace.

Think Good Thoughts
on Purpose

And be constantly renewed in the spirit of your
mind [having a fresh mental and spiritual attitude].

EPHESIANS 4:23

We know that when God has renewed our mind with a fresh attitude we can choose to make right decisions. For instance, we know that love is not necessarily a feeling but a choice. We must also choose to think good thoughts about other people. Take a moment and think good thoughts about someone you know, and see how much better you feel.

Thinking good thoughts opens the door for God to manifest His good plan in your life. So if you haven't been working with the Holy Spirit to break old thought patterns and form new ones, it's time to get started. Think good thoughts about people on purpose, and as your attitude starts to change toward others, your relationships will also start to change for the better.

An Ant's Life

But [like a boxer] I buffet my body [handle it
roughly, discipline it by hardships] and subdue it,
for fear that after proclaiming to others the Gospel
and things pertaining to it, I myself should become
unfit [not stand the test, be unapproved and
rejected as a counterfeit].

I CORINTHIANS 9:27

Paul is speaking here about self-control, self-denial, restraining the appetite, and subduing the flesh. Self-discipline is keeping yourself going in the right direction without someone making you do so. The problem is that somehow people have gotten the wrong idea that everything in life is supposed to be easy.

Proverbs 6:6-8 talks about the ant, "which having no chief, overseer, or ruler, provides her food in the summer and gathers her supplies in the harvest." You need to be like the ant. You need to be a person who is self-motivated and self-disciplined; who does what is right because it is right, not because someone may be looking or because someone is making you do it.

Be a Friend of God

And [so] the Scripture was fulfilled that says,
Abraham believed in (adhered to, trusted in, and
relied on) God, and this was accounted to him as
righteousness (as conformity to God's will in thought
and deed), and he was called God's friend.

JAMES 2:23

It's obvious some people are closer to God than others. These "close friends" of God speak of talking to Him as if they know Him personally. Their faces shine with enthusiasm as they testify, "And God told me . . ." while skeptical acquaintances grumble to themselves, "Well, God doesn't talk to me like that!"

Why is that? Does God have favorites? No, Scripture teaches that each person determines his or her own level of intimacy with God, depending on their willingness to seek Him and put time into developing a relationship with Him. Everyone has been extended the same open invitation to "fearlessly and confidently and boldly draw near to the throne of grace" (Hebrews 4:16). At this moment, you are as close to God as you choose to be.

Handling Criticism

*And so each of us shall give an account of himself
[give an answer in reference to judgment] to God.*

ROMANS 14:12

We crave acceptance, therefore criticism
and judgment are hard on us mentally
and emotionally. The fact is—it hurts! But con-
fronting the criticism and judgment of other people
becomes easier when you remember that ultimately
it is before your own master you stand or fall (see
Romans 14:4). In the end you will answer to God
alone.

Criticism and judgment are the devil's tools. He
uses them to stop people from fulfilling their destiny
and to steal their liberty and creativity. Paul did not
allow the opinions of others to change his destiny. In
Galatians 1:10 he said if he had been seeking popularity with people, he would not have become an
apostle of the Lord Jesus Christ. This statement
contains important wisdom. How can we succeed at
what God has called us to if we are overly concerned
about what other people think?

Realistic Expectations

In the world you have tribulation and trials and
distress and frustration; but be of good cheer [take
courage; be confident, certain, undaunted]! For I have
overcome the world. [I have deprived it of power to
harm you and have conquered it for you.]

JOHN 16:33

If you get the idea in your head that everything concerning your life should always be perfect, you are setting yourself up for a fall. This is not to suggest you should be negative. But you do need to be realistic enough to realize ahead of time that very few things in life are ever perfect.

You should not plan for failure, but you do need to remember Jesus said you will have to deal with tribulation and trials and distress and frustration. These things are part of life on this earth—for the believer as well as the unbeliever. But all the mishaps in the world cannot harm you if you will remain in the love of God.

Faith for the Miracle

> *And there was a woman who had had a flow of*
> *blood for twelve years, and who had endured much*
> *suffering under [the hands of] many physicians and*
> *had spent all that she had, and was no better but*
> *instead grew worse. She had heard the reports con-*
> *cerning Jesus, and she came up behind Him in the*
> *throng and touched His garment.*
>
> MARK 5:25-27

Surely this woman must have been attacked with thoughts of hopelessness. When she considered going to Jesus she must have thought, "What's the use?" But she pressed forward through the thick, suffocating crowd and touched the hem of Jesus' garment. Healing virtue flowed to her and she was made well.

No matter what she felt like, no matter how much others tried to discourage her, even though she had suffered for twelve years, this woman did not give up. Jesus told her it was her faith that had made her whole. Keep pressing forward—and don't give up hope!

The Path of Forgiveness

*And whenever you stand praying, if you have
anything against anyone, forgive him and let it drop
(leave it, let it go), in order that your Father Who is
in heaven may also forgive you your [own] failings
and shortcomings and let them drop.*

MARK 11:25

"Why me, God?" was the cry of my heart
for many years. Because of my wounded
emotions from a lifetime of suffering, I lived in a
wilderness of self-pity and unforgiveness. It was a
huge problem that kept me from fulfilling the plan
of God for my life.

Many people are hurting terribly and are crying
out for help, but they aren't willing to receive the
help God has to offer. It is amazing how often we
want things our way. When someone hurts you, you
may feel they owe you something, yet Jesus wants
you to let it go. No matter how much you may want
His help, you will receive only when you become
willing to do things God's way.

Ask for Help

The Lord says this to you: Be not afraid or dismayed at this great multitude; for the battle is not yours, but God's.

2 CHRONICLES 20:15

The twentieth chapter of 2 Chronicles describes a time of crisis in the life of the people of Judah. They were faced with a huge army that was out to destroy them. In verse 12, Jehoshaphat, king of Judah, offered a wise prayer to God: "O our God, will You not exercise judgment upon them? For we have no might to stand against this great company that is coming against us. We do not know what to do, but our eyes are upon You."

Often we spin our wheels trying to do something we are not capable of doing. It is much easier to just say, "I don't know what to do, and even if I did, I couldn't do it without Your help. Holy Spirit, help me!" If you ask for help, God will take care of the battle.

Develop Your Potential

*Whatever your hand finds to do,
do it with all your might.*
ECCLESIASTES 9:10

Webster's 1828 *American Dictionary of the English Language* defines *potential* as "existing in possibility, not in act." Potential cannot manifest without form. Like concrete it must have something to be poured into, something to give it shape and make it useful. To develop potential properly you must have a plan and pray over that plan, you must have a purpose, and you must be doing something.

Many people are unhappy because they aren't doing anything to develop their potential. In fact, many of them never develop their potential because they don't do anything except complain that they're not doing anything!

If you want to see your potential developed to its fullness, don't wait until everything is perfect. Do something now. Start laying your hand to whatever is in front of you. You cannot start at the finish line. You must start at the beginning like everybody else.

Quick to Love, Slow to Judge

*And walk in love, [esteeming and delighting
in one another] as Christ loved us and
gave Himself up for us.*

EPHESIANS 5:2

You are instructed to walk in love. To esteem and delight yourself in others, you have to first get to know others, which is an act of love. It takes time and effort to look beyond the surface of any human being. Too often, we are tempted to judge hastily, but the Word says, "Be honest in your judgment and do not decide at a glance (superficially and by appearances); but judge fairly and righteously" (John 7:24).

Before you judge an individual, you must take time to get to know the real person. Everyone has their little quirks, oddball actions, behaviors, and imperfections. God Himself does not judge by appearance—He looks on the heart. You should follow His example. As the saying goes, "never judge a book by its cover"!

Fellowship with the Father

Even when we were dead (slain) by [our own]
shortcomings and trespasses, He made us alive
together in fellowship and in union with Christ.

EPHESIANS 2:5

Fellowship ministers life to you. You are renewed by it. It charges your batteries, so to speak. You are made strong through union and fellowship with God—strong enough to withstand the attacks of the enemy of your soul, who is Satan (see Ephesians 6:10-11).

When you are fellowshipping with God, you are in a secret place where you are protected from the enemy. Psalm 91 talks of this secret place, and the first verse says that those who dwell there will defeat every foe: "He who dwells in the secret place of the Most High shall remain stable and fixed under the shadow of the Almighty [Whose power no foe can withstand]" (Psalm 91:1). This secret place is God's presence. When you are in His presence, you experience His peace. Tonight, as you pray and fellowship with God, enter the holy of holies and rest in the secret place of His Presence.

An Eternal Perspective

But the day of the Lord will come like a thief, and then the heavens will vanish (pass away) with a thunderous crash, and the [material] elements [of the universe] will be dissolved with fire, and the earth and the works that are upon it will be burned up. Since all these things are thus in the process of being dissolved, what kind of person ought [each of] you to be [in the meanwhile] in consecrated and holy behavior and devout and godly qualities, while you wait and earnestly long for (expect and hasten) the coming of the day of God? . . . Be eager to be found by Him [at His coming] without spot or blemish and at peace [in serene confidence, free from fears and agitating passions and moral conflicts].

2 PETER 3:10-12,14

This passage of Scripture should invoke reverential fear and awe within you. It is a waste of time trying to impress people—what matters is what God thinks of you. You must keep an eternal perspective. The world as we know it will one day vanish and Jesus will return. We should spend our time in this world preparing ourselves to enjoy eternity in God's Presence.

At Home in Your Heart

May Christ through your faith [actually]
dwell (settle down, abide, make His permanent
home) in your hearts!
EPHESIANS 3:17

If you are born again Jesus dwells on the inside of you. Your inner life—your attitudes, thoughts, and emotions—is holy ground where the Spirit of God wants to make His home. This inner life is of more serious interest to God than your outer life.

If you want to be a comfortable home for God, you must give up grumbling and faultfinding. The Bible says God inhabits the praises of His people (see Psalm 22:3). He is comfortable in the midst of your praises. You need to wake up every morning and say, "Oh, good morning Jesus. I want You to be comfortable in me today." And you need to go to bed every night and say, "Thank You for all the good things You've done today and will be doing tomorrow." Before you do anything else, invite Jesus to make Himself at home in your heart. Then go forward confidently, enjoying the God-kind of life.

Heirs with Christ

Therefore, you are no longer a slave (bond servant)
but a son; and if a son, then [it follows that you are]
an heir by the aid of God, through Christ.

GALATIANS 4:7

As a Christian, you believe Jesus died for your sins and that when you die you will go to heaven because you believe in Him. But there is more to our redemption than that. There is a life of victory God wants for you now.

It is impossible to live victoriously in this earth without understanding your rightful authority and dominion over the devil and all his works. Your position "in Christ" is one of being seated at the right hand of the Lord God Omnipotent.

God wants to restore you to the place of authority that is yours. He has already made all the arrangements; you might say He has "sealed the deal." The purchase price has been paid in full. You have been bought by the precious blood of Jesus. Therefore, I encourage you to go forth with confidence and enjoy the life Jesus has provided for you.

Something Good

We have thought of Your steadfast love,
O God, in the midst of Your temple.

PSALM 48:9

David wrote often about the wonderful works of God. When he was feeling depressed he wrote in Psalm 143:4-5, "Therefore is my spirit overwhelmed and faints within me [wrapped in gloom]; my heart within my bosom grows numb. I remember the days of old; I meditate on all Your doings; I ponder the work of Your hands." David's response to his feelings of depression and gloom was to choose to remember the good times of past days—pondering the doings of God and the works of His hands. In other words, he thought on something good, and it helped him overcome depression.

When the enemy comes against you with depression or discouragement, choose to remember the times God has blessed and delivered you in the past. Hope will rise in your heart and your troubles will seem small.

Submit to Suffering

*So, since Christ suffered in the flesh for us, for you,
arm yourselves with the same thought and purpose
[patiently to suffer rather than fail to please God].*

I PETER 4:1

It is important to understand the difference between suffering in the flesh and suffering demonic affliction. Giving up the selfish appetites of our flesh does not mean we are to suffer from sickness, disease, and poverty. Jesus died to deliver you from the curse of sin. But unless you are willing to suffer in the flesh you will never walk in the will of God.

When you get up in the morning, set your thoughts on walking in God's will all day long. You might even say to yourself, "Even if I need to suffer in order to do God's will today, I am setting my mind for obedience." Tonight, purpose in your heart that you will face tomorrow with determination to please God no matter the cost.

One Step at a Time

For our knowledge is fragmentary (incomplete and imperfect), and our prophecy (our teaching) is fragmentary (incomplete and imperfect). But when the complete and perfect (total) comes, the incomplete and imperfect will vanish away (become antiquated, void, and superseded).

1 CORINTHIANS 13:9-10

This scripture says that as long as you are on this earth, until Jesus comes, there will never be a time in your life when you can say, "I have every answer for my life right now, I know everything about everything." God requires us to trust Him and trust requires unanswered questions.

Like I once did, you may think you know it all! But you know in part, and that is why trust is still needed no matter how long you have walked with God. He leads you. He doesn't hand you a map and send you on your way without Him. God wants you to keep your eyes on Him, and follow Him one step at a time.

Comfort for Mourning

You have turned my mourning into dancing for
me; You have put off my sackcloth and
girded me with gladness.

PSALM 30:11

In Isaiah 61:2 it was prophesied that the coming Messiah would "comfort all who mourn." In the Sermon on the Mount, Jesus said those who mourn are blessed for they will be comforted (see Matthew 5:4). The comfort of God that is administered by His Holy Spirit is so awesome it is almost worth having a problem just to be able to experience it. It goes far beyond any kind of ordinary human comfort.

Let God be your source of comfort. In those times when you are hurting, just ask Him to comfort you. Then wait in His presence while He works in your heart and emotions. He will not fail you, if you will only give Him a chance to come to your aid.

Words of Purpose

So shall My word be that goes forth out of My mouth: it shall not return to Me void [without producing any effect, useless], but it shall accomplish that which I please and purpose, and it shall prosper in the thing for which I sent it.

ISAIAH 55:11

The prophets were mouthpieces for God. They were called to speak God's words to people, situations, cities, dry bones, mountains, or whatever God told them to speak to. To fulfill their God-ordained mission they had to be submitted to the Lord—their mouth had to be His.

If you desire the words of your mouth to carry God's power, your mouth must belong to Him. Usually people who have "verbal" gifts also have some glaring weaknesses in the area of their mouth. If you desire to be used by God you need to allow Him to deal with you concerning your mouth and what comes out of it. When you speak His words they will accomplish their purpose and will never return void.

Choose to Forgive

*[Now having received the Holy Spirit, and
being led and directed by Him] if you forgive the
sins of anyone, they are forgiven; if you retain
the sins of anyone, they are retained.*

JOHN 20:23

The greatest deception Satan has perpetuated in the area of forgiveness is the idea that if your feelings have not changed, you have not truly forgiven. Many people believe this lie. They decide to forgive someone who has harmed them, but the devil convinces them that because they still have the same feelings, they have not really forgiven the person.

You can make the right decision to forgive and not feel any differently. This is where faith is needed to carry you through. You have done your part and now you are waiting on God. His part is to heal your emotions, to make you feel well and whole. Only God has the power to change your feelings toward the person who hurt you.

Always Constant

Jesus Christ (the Messiah) is [always] the same,
yesterday, today, [yes] and forever (to the ages).

HEBREWS 13:8

What is the main thing you love so much about Jesus? There are many answers to that question, of course, such as the fact He died for you on the cross so you wouldn't have to be punished for your sins; then He rose again on the third day. But in your daily relationship with Him, one of the things you will appreciate most about Him is the fact you can count on Him not to change.

You love Jesus and are able to trust Him because He is never changing. He has said in His Word, "This is the way I was, and this is the way I'm always going to be." If you can count on anything, you can count on Jesus never changing. He can change anything else that needs to be changed, but He always remains constant.

Ending Your Day Right ~ 233

The Scarlet Cord

*[Prompted] by faith Rahab the prostitute was
not destroyed along with those who refused to
believe and obey, because she had received
the spies in peace [without enmity].*

HEBREWS 11:31

Rahab hid the spies whom Joshua had sent in to spy out the land. Because of her they were kept safe from the king who would have killed them. Before their departure she asked them to protect her just as she had protected them. These men told her, "Stay under the scarlet cord, and you will be safe. Not only you, but all those of your family whom you bring in with you. But if anyone gets out from under the protection of the scarlet cord, he will be destroyed" (see Joshua 2). Rahab obeyed their instructions and was saved from destruction (see Joshua 6:25).

The scarlet cord represents the blood of Jesus—which runs throughout the Bible. Use the blood of Jesus as a marker over you and your family. When God sees it, He will pass over you.

Stronger by Faith

The Lord is my Strength and my Song, and He has become my Salvation; this is my God, and I will praise Him, my father's God, and I will exalt Him.

EXODUS 15:2

God does not want to just give you strength; He wants to *be* your strength. In 1 Samuel 15:29 God is referred to as the Strength of Israel. There was a time when Israel knew God was their strength. But when they forgot it, they always started to fail and their lives began to be filled with destruction.

How do you receive strength from God? By faith. Hebrews 11:11 says that by faith Sarah received strength to conceive a child when she was well past childbearing age. By faith you can receive strength to stay in a difficult marriage, raise a difficult child, or prosper in a difficult job. Start receiving God as your strength by faith. It will quicken your body as well as your spirit and soul.

A Powerful Compass

And let the peace (soul harmony which comes) from
Christ rule (act as umpire continually) in your hearts
[deciding and settling with finality all questions
that arise in your minds, in that peaceful state]
to which as [members of Christ's] one body
you were also called [to live].

COLOSSIANS 3:15

People who do things they don't have peace about have miserable lives and don't succeed at anything. If you are doing something, like watching television, and you suddenly lose your peace about what you are watching, you have heard from God. He is saying to you, "Turn it off. Go the other way." If you lose your peace when you say something unkind, God is speaking to you. It will save you a lot of trouble if you will stop talking or apologize right away.

God leads His people through peace. Anytime you lose your peace you are hearing from God. There is nothing more powerful than the compass of peace in your heart. Follow after it. Follow peace!

Pray for Blessing

*Invoke blessings upon and pray for the happiness
of those who curse you, implore God's blessing (favor)
upon those who abuse you [who revile, reproach,
disparage, and high-handedly misuse you].*

LUKE 6:28

A common misconception is that all you
have to do if you are wronged is make the
decision to forgive and your job is finished. But God
also says, "Bless those who persecute you [who are
cruel in their attitude toward you]; bless and do not
curse them" (Romans 12:14).

In this context the word *bless* means "to speak
well of." It is extending mercy to people who do not
deserve it. Not only are you to extend forgiveness to
those who hurt you, you are to pray for them to be
blessed spiritually. You are to ask God to bring truth
and revelation so they will be willing to repent and
be set free from their sins. Don't just forgive—
complete the process by asking God to bless them.
He will bless you greatly for your obedience.

The Unseen Foe

For we are not wrestling with flesh and blood
[contending only with physical opponents], but
against the despotisms, against the powers, against
[the master spirits who are] the world rulers of
this present darkness, against the spirit forces of
wickedness in the heavenly (supernatural) sphere.

EPHESIANS 6:12

This verse points out that you war not with other human beings, but against the devil and his demons. Your enemy, Satan, attempts to defeat you with strategy and deceit, through well-laid plans and deliberate deception.

The devil is a liar. Jesus called him "the father of lies and of all that is false" (John 8:44). He tells you things about yourself, about other people, and about circumstances that are just not true. He begins by bombarding your mind with little nagging doubts and fears. He moves slowly and cautiously. He knows your insecurities and fears. He has studied you for a long time. But remember the greater One lives in you. You cannot be defeated if you trust God to keep you safe.

Chosen and Adopted

*Even as [in His love] He chose us [actually picked
us out for Himself as His own] in Christ before the
foundation of the world, that we should be holy
(consecrated and set apart for Him) and blameless in
His sight, even above reproach, before Him in love.
For He foreordained us (destined us, planned in love
for us) to be adopted (revealed) as His own children
through Jesus Christ, in accordance with the
purpose of His will [because it pleased
Him and was His kind intent].*

EPHESIANS 1:4-5

You understand adoption in the natural
sense. You know some children without
parents are adopted by people who purposely choose
them and raise them as their own. In the same way
you have been chosen and brought into the family of
God even though you were previously an outsider,
unrelated to God in any way. God in His great
mercy redeemed you and purchased you with the
blood of His own Son, and He has provided an inheritance that is wonderful beyond understanding.
God has many good things in His plan for you so
start expecting blessings!

Be a Peacemaker

*Blessed (enjoying enviable happiness, spiritually
prosperous—with life-joy and satisfaction in God's
favor and salvation, regardless of their outward
conditions) are the makers and maintainers of
peace, for they shall be called the sons of God!*

MATTHEW 5:9

Jesus is the King of Peace. You are called
to be a maker and maintainer of peace. If
you are going to serve the Lord you cannot live in
strife. God did not merely suggest you not be in
strife—it is His command: "The servant of the Lord
must not strive" (2 Timothy 2:24 KJV).

Being a peacemaker is a decision, but not all are
willing because it's not always easy. When you decide to be a peacemaker does that mean you must
submit passively to mistreatment from others? Does
it mean you can never give your opinion or let
someone know how you feel? Not at all! It means
you hold your peace in upsetting and frustrating situations, because of your love and devotion to the
Lord. Even though it is often challenging, choose to
walk in peace and you will be blessed.

The Price of Ishmael

Now Sarai, Abram's wife, had borne him no children. She had an Egyptian maid whose name was Hagar. And Sarai said to Abram, See here, the Lord has restrained me from bearing [children]. I am asking you to have intercourse with my maid; it may be that I can obtain children by her. And Abram listened to and heeded what Sarai said.

GENESIS 16:1-2

Abraham and Sarah got tired of waiting on God. They wondered if there was something they could do to help move things along. The result was the birth of a child named Ishmael. But Ishmael was not the child of promise.

Like all of us, you probably like to do your own thing, but God is not obligated to take care of those things you give birth to in the strength of your own flesh. There are many frustrated people who have given birth to "Ishmaels." God did not say you should not build. But He did say, "Except the Lord builds the house, they labor in vain who build it" (Psalm 127:1). Make sure what you do is led by the Holy Spirit and not a fleshly desire.

Facing Persecution

*Remember that I told you, A servant is not greater
than his master [is not superior to him]. If they
persecuted Me, they will also persecute you.*

JOHN 15:20

People will reject you just as they rejected Jesus and Paul and the other apostles and disciples. It is especially difficult when you are persecuted by people who are living wrong and are saying wrong things about you. Psalm 118:22 says, "The stone which the builders rejected has become the chief cornerstone." This passage is talking about David who was rejected by the Jewish rulers, but later was chosen by the Lord to be the ruler of Israel. In Matthew 21:42 Jesus quoted this verse to the chief priests and the Pharisees, referring to their rejection of Him as the Son of God.

Even though people may reject you, if you will hold steady and continue to do what God is telling you to do with a good attitude, God will promote you and place you where no man can put you.

Think on These Things

*Whatever is true, whatever is worthy of reverence
and is honorable and seemly, whatever is just, whatever is pure, whatever is lovely and lovable, whatever
is kind and winsome and gracious, if there is any
virtue and excellence, if there is anything worthy
of praise, think on and weigh and take account
of these things [fix your minds on them].*

PHILIPPIANS 4:8

Many years ago my philosophy was, "Don't expect anything good to happen, and then you won't be disappointed when it doesn't." Since my thoughts were negative, so was my life.

Perhaps this describes you. You avoid hope to protect yourself against being hurt. Unfortunately this type of behavior sets up a negative lifestyle where everything seems to go wrong.

Maintain a positive outlook and attitude. Speak positive words. Jesus endured tremendous difficulties and yet He remained positive. He always had an uplifting comment, an encouraging word. You have the mind of Christ, so begin to use it. If He wouldn't think it, you shouldn't think it either.

Be a Doer

But be doers of the Word [obey the message], and not merely listeners to it, betraying yourselves [into deception by reasoning contrary to the Truth].

JAMES 1:22

Any time you see what the Word says and refuse to do it, reasoning has somehow gotten involved and deceived you into believing something other than the truth. There may be times when you don't understand everything the Word says, but you should move ahead and do it. God wants you to obey him whether or not you feel like it, want to do it, or think it is a good idea. When God speaks, we are not to question His methods. His ways are not our own.

Proverbs 3:5 says, "Lean on, trust in, and be confident in the Lord with all your heart and mind and do not rely on your own insight or understanding." In other words, don't rely on reason or logic. When God speaks, we are to mobilize, not rationalize.

You Have the Mind of Christ

We have the mind of Christ (the Messiah)
and do hold the thoughts (feelings and
purposes) of His heart.

1 CORINTHIANS 2:16

The Bible clearly tells you that as a Christian you have the mind of Christ. Why, then, do you experience times when you feel like you're on an emotional roller coaster?

Romans 8 teaches that you also have a mind of the flesh, which causes you to think, say, feel, and do things that make you unproductive.

That's why it's important to recognize your feelings are not reliable. You must choose to go deeper than your feelings and live by what you know deep in your heart.

If you sometimes feel your mind is lost in a maze of confusion, it's time to give up the mind of the flesh and operate in the mind of Christ. It is an exchange that will lead you out of frustration and into victorious Christian living.

Be a Light in a Dark World

By this shall all [men] know that you are My
disciples, if you love one another [if you keep
on showing love among yourselves].

JOHN 13:35

You have the opportunity every day to show Jesus to the world. You do that by walking in His love—the love of the Father that was first revealed and expressed in His Son Jesus and is now manifested in you.

The world is looking for something real, something tangible. They are looking for love, and God is the source of all love.

According to 2 Corinthians 5:20 you are Christ's ambassador, His personal representative. God is making His appeal to the world through you.

Do people sense you love and care about them? Does the way you live your life make them desire to have a relationship with God? Be a light in the dark places of the world.

Think Before You Speak

Set a guard, O Lord, before my mouth;
keep watch at the door of my lips.

PSALM 141:3

Have you ever said something that hurt someone else . . . or perhaps caused unfavorable consequences for yourself?

I know I have. For years I just said whatever I felt like saying, but thank God I have learned that words are powerful. What you say has the power to impact your life—and the lives of others—for good or bad. So it is wise to think about what you're going to say before you say it.

You should speak only words of encouragement that will build people up and make them feel better. You get many opportunities every day to put this into practice, but it requires real discipline and determination.

You may have been hurt by someone's words . . . or perhaps you have hurt someone with your words. But you can change that, starting now. It will take prayer and discipline, but God will help you develop and exercise control over the words you speak.

Pursue Your Purpose

But seek (aim at and strive after) first of all His kingdom and His righteousness (His way of doing and being right), and then all these things taken together will be given you besides.

MATTHEW 6:33

Have you ever thought, "What is my purpose in life?" Each of us wants to feel we have a purpose . . . that we're making a meaningful difference in the world.

God has a purpose for each of us, and that is to do right and glorify God.

How do you pursue your purpose? By getting up each day and putting God first. There are many other things we may be tempted to chase after—job position, education, relationships, money, material possessions, and so on. But too often when you attain these things your life is just as empty and unfulfilled as when you started.

God knows what you need and is well aware of your heart's desires, and He will grant them if you will just pursue your purpose by seeking Him first.

Enjoy Your Life Now

*I came that they may have and enjoy life, and
have it in abundance (to the full, till it overflows).*

JOHN 10:10

Life is a journey—a process of advancement and progression. And as you move toward the future, you must be careful not to lose sight of the now and the enjoyment it can bring you.

For many years I was a Christian but not enjoying life. Then God taught me that enjoying life is not based on enjoyable circumstances. It is an attitude of the heart. When I decided to change my approach to some of the circumstances I faced in life, it made a remarkable difference!

As a believer you have available to you the abundant quality of life that comes from God. Don't get so caught up in your busyness that you fail to enjoy the pleasures God provides every day. He has given you abundant life and your goal should be to enjoy it to the fullest.

Let Your Light Shine

*The grace of God . . . has trained us to reject
and renounce all ungodliness (irreligion) and worldly
(passionate) desires, to live discreet (temperate,
self-controlled), upright, devout (spiritually
whole) lives in this present world.*

TITUS 2:11-12

Although you live in the world, you are not to be of the world . . . worldly in your ways. Because it is easy to become worldly without realizing it, you need the godly influence of spiritually mature people in your life. You also need to be a student of God's Word, which can change your ungodly desires and train and establish godly character in you.

As a child of God, you are to be a light to others who dwell in darkness. People should be able to tell by your joy, the light in your eyes, the way you treat people, the way you talk about people—or don't talk about them—that you are a Christian.

Determine now that you will be a light in this present world. Ask God to help you glorify Him through your choices and actions.

Pursue a Life of Excellence

Don't look for shortcuts to God. The market is
flooded with surefire, easygoing formulas for a
successful life that can be practiced in your spare
time. Don't fall for that stuff, even though crowds
of people do. The way to life—to God!—is
vigorous and requires total attention.

MATTHEW 7:13-14 THE MESSAGE

Many people are trapped in a mediocre lifestyle. They seem to lack personal motivation, so they are easy targets for those who promise an easy way to success that requires little effort on their part. They do just enough to get by, but they never go the extra mile.

Living that kind of life is a poor substitute for the real rewards in life that can only be found in being a person of excellence, which was God's plan for you from the beginning.

Learn the truth about God's good plan for your life and vigorously pursue it. You will sense a wonderful fulfillment and the fruit of your life will be abundant and bring glory to God.

Face the Truth and Find Freedom

But when He, the Spirit of Truth (the Truth-giving Spirit) comes, He will guide you into all the Truth.

JOHN 16:13

Facing the truth about yourself is a vital key to experiencing a breakthrough to victory. If you want to continually live in new levels of victory, you must remain open and receptive to the truth about yourself. This is not just a superficial acknowledgment of wrong thinking and behavior—it is an open and honest recognition of your sin before God that brings an attitude of repentance, which is a willingness to go in the right direction.

It can be painful, but facing the truth about your mindsets, motives, and methods of doing things enables you to move beyond your despair and experience a wonderful fellowship with God.

The truth about yourself often brings great hurt, but the truth of God's Word brings great healing. As you continue in His Word, the truth will set you free (see John 8:32).

Exercise the Privilege of Prayer

Pray at all times (on every occasion, in every season) in the Spirit, with all [manner of] prayer.

EPHESIANS 6:18

Prayer to many is just a ritual reserved for church services or special occasions. To others, it is something they do when they have a problem or get sick. But prayer is not some ritual or mechanical function. It is something you should live out all day long, just like breathing.

Prayer is conversation with God, and effective prayer includes thanksgiving, praise, and petitions. And it works for all kinds of situations, from small to great . . . and at any time of day or night.

Prayer demonstrates humility; it's a symbol of your dependence upon God. And the humble get the help.

As you settle down to sleep tonight, pray and let God know how much you love Him. Thank Him, praise Him, and offer any petitions you may have, knowing He hears and answers prayer. Then enjoy a peaceful night of rest.

Live and Let Live

Make it your ambition and definitely endeavor to live quietly and peacefully, to mind your own affairs, and to work with your hands.

1 THESSALONIANS 4:11

The phrase *live and let live* means "you mind your business, and I'll mind mine—and vice versa." And the Bible confirms this is a good practice. I have discovered that the application of this principle aids me greatly in enjoying my life.

Many times we get into things that are really none of our business, and sometimes those things make us miserable. I encourage you not to become entangled with the lives of others. Be a good friend, but beware of entanglements. It is possible to lose yourself in someone else's life, but that is not God's plan for you.

Most of us have enough business of our own, without getting involved in the business of others. So make it your ambition to mind your own business and endeavor to live quietly and peacefully. It's a great way to live!

Just Believe

May the God of your hope so fill you with all
joy and peace in believing . . . that by the power
of the Holy Spirit you may abound and be
overflowing (bubbling over) with hope.

ROMANS 15:13

As a believer, your joy and peace are not based on doing and achieving, but on believing. Joy and peace come as a result of building your relationship with the Lord.

Psalm 16:11 tells you that in His presence is fullness of joy. If you have received Jesus as your Savior and Lord, He—the Prince of Peace—lives inside you (see John 14:23; 1 John 4:12-15). You experience peace in the Lord's presence, receiving from Him and acting in response to His direction.

Joy and peace come from knowing, believing, and trusting in the Lord with simple childlike faith. So just believe . . . and be filled with an overflowing hope that cascades into every area of your life.

Experience God's Presence Tonight

My soul yearns for You [O Lord] in the night,
yes, my spirit within me seeks You earnestly.

ISAIAH 26:9

Have you ever noticed that in the quiet darkness of night there seems to be something special about the presence of God?

He is always with you, even during the daytime, and you can talk to Him anytime, even when you're busy. But during the day there are many distractions that keep you from focusing on His presence for an extended period of time. And by the end of the day you've often experienced problems and frustrations that can cause you to feel lonely and needy. It is then that you can finally give time and attention to the one who is the answer to your needs.

When you yearn for God in the night, seek Him earnestly, and you'll find He will minister to you in a special way. He will provide answers to any problems you may have, and He will give you peace and rest.

Speak Words of Wisdom

For out of the fullness (the overflow, the super-abundance) of the heart the mouth speaks.

MATTHEW 12:34

It is challenging to say right things when you feel totally wrong. When your emotions are running high or low, you are tempted to speak emotionally rather than sensibly. But you must allow wisdom to rise above emotion.

God spoke about nonexistent things as if they already existed, and He created the world with faith-filled words. You are created in His image, and you can also call things that are not as though they are. You can speak positive things about yourself into the atmosphere and thereby "prophesy your future."

Think about the words you speak and you will learn a lot about yourself. As a Christian, you are God's representative, and your words should reflect His character. Meditating on the goodness of God will fill your heart with joy, and the words you speak will glorify Him and be a testimony to others.

Learn How to Fly

*Those who wait for the Lord . . . shall change and
renew their strength . . . they shall lift their wings
and mount up [close to God] as eagles . . . they
shall run and not be weary, they shall walk
and not faint or become tired.*

ISAIAH 40:31

God's Word makes several references to eagles, the most powerful winged creature on earth, and I believe you can learn some valuable lessons from them.

Eagles do not fear or run from a storm—they allow the powerful wind currents to lift them above it. Nor do they waste time battling with other birds. When attacked, they simply mount up higher, soaring effortlessly above their enemies.

When you grow weary of the struggles and battles of the "lower life," it's time to learn to fly.

Allow God to teach you how to fly above your problems. Be determined to know Him and the power of His resurrection. You'll discover that when you're soaring close to the heart of God, you can face whatever comes without growing tired and weary.

Take Up the Easy Yoke

Take My yoke upon you and learn of Me, for I am
gentle (meek) and humble (lowly) in heart, and you
will find rest (relief and ease and refreshment and
recreation and blessed quiet) for your souls.

MATTHEW 11:29

There is a life that is so superior to anything the world has to offer that no comparison can be made. But in order to have that kind of life you must be willing to be yoked to Christ and learn His ways. This means you must stay close to Him and learn how He handles every situation that arises.

His ways and thoughts are far superior to yours, and you must be willing to abandon yourself to Him and discover what His will is for your life.

Give up being independent and learn to lean and depend on God. Give Him full reign of your life. In return you will find rest, relief, ease, refreshment, recreation, and blessed quiet.

Pray About Everything

The earnest (heartfelt, continued) prayer of a
righteous man makes tremendous power available
[dynamic in its working].

JAMES 5:16

Driving down the road one day, pondering an upcoming change in my life, I found that I was afraid. It really wasn't a major thing, but it felt like it to me.

God spoke to me that day and simply said, "Pray about everything. Fear nothing." He showed me He couldn't work through my fear, but if I would give Him my faith, He would help me in my situation. I needed it that day for something seemingly minor, but I have used it many times since for all types of situations.

Isn't it good to know that God cares about everything that concerns you—even the little things you're afraid of? Your part is to pray and have faith, and God's part is to provide the power to meet your need. What do you need to pray about tonight?

Grace for the Humble

But He gives us more and more grace (power of the Holy Spirit, to meet [our] evil tendency). That is why He says, God sets Himself against the proud and haughty, but gives grace [continually] to the lowly (those who are humble enough to receive it).

JAMES 4:6

All human beings have evil tendencies, but if you are humble enough to ask for and receive God's grace, He will give it to you.

Early in my Christian life I tried to take care of my own evil tendencies, but I was not successful. God opposed all my fleshly "Joyce" plans. I finally learned that the proud try to take care of themselves, but the humble lean on God and get the help.

If you have tried to make things happen in your own strength you are probably frustrated like I once was. But I encourage you to do what I did—trust in the grace and power of the Holy Spirit . . . and receive everything you need from Him.

Plant Your Trust in God

[Most] blessed is the man who believes in, trusts in, and relies on the Lord, and whose hope and confidence the Lord is. For he shall be like a tree planted by the waters that spreads out its roots by the river . . . It shall not be anxious and full of care in the year of drought, nor shall it cease yielding fruit.

JEREMIAH 17:7-8

Trust is one of the most powerful facets of faith because it carries you through your problems. Faith asks for deliverance, but trust remains steadfast while we are in God's waiting room.

We all have trust, and we choose where we place that trust. If you place your trust in others or in your own abilities and accomplishments, you will one day be disappointed. All of these things are subject to change. But God never changes.

So plant your trust in Him and be like the tree planted by the water—rooted and grounded and yielding good fruit no matter what comes.

You Are More Than
a Conqueror

Yet amid all these things we are more than
conquerors and gain a surpassing victory
through Him Who loved us.

ROMANS 8:37

Some people believe the only way to victory is to somehow avoid having problems. But I have learned that real victory is not in being problem free. True victory for the child of God comes when there is still peace in the soul right in the midst of the raging storm—when tragedy strikes and one can still say, "It is well with my soul." This can only happen when you are looking at Jesus instead of your circumstances.

The key to having victory is understanding it only comes "through Him who loved us." If you are facing problems that seem insurmountable, remember you are a conqueror through Him. Allow God to strengthen your inner man. When you are strong inside you can defeat anything that comes against you.

Invest in a Pure Heart

Blessed are the pure in heart: for they shall see God.

MATTHEW 5:8 KJV

Purity of heart is not a natural trait—it is something that must be worked in you. I believe purging and purity go together. Purging is a tedious process in which worthless things are removed while the things of value are retained. Removing the worthless without harming the valuable requires an expert—and God is an expert!

He's like the refiner who sits over the fire where gold and silver are being refined. He never leaves you for one second, but watches over you, and when impurities are being extracted He makes sure the valuable things in you are not harmed.

God was willing to pay the price to redeem you. Are you willing to pay the price to have purity in your life—purity of motives, thoughts, attitudes, words, and actions? Think of more than the moment. What feels good now may bring destruction later. But what seems costly now will pay rich rewards.

Hold Fast to Your Dream

*A dream comes with much business and
painful effort.*

ECCLESIASTES 5:3

In a fast-paced world that is both challenging and demanding it is important to have dreams and visions. Without them it is easy to become complacent and fail to grow beyond where you are right now. However, working toward your dreams and visions requires hard work.

Those who want to do great things without having to work hard will never see it come to pass. Using good business principles and being willing to work are requirements in the kingdom of God.

Walking in kindness and love is a major factor in seeing your dreams fulfilled. No person is an island to himself—we need other people to help us be all we can be. Therefore we must operate with principles that build good relationships.

As you hold fast to the dreams God has placed in your heart, prayerfully seek His guidance, and He will lead you to miraculous victories in your life.

Enjoy Life as You Grow

You, therefore, must be perfect [growing into complete maturity of godliness in mind and character, having reached the proper height of virtue and integrity], as your heavenly Father is perfect.

MATTHEW 5:48

Being perfect sounds good, but it is not reality. Reality is that you are a human being, and no matter how hard you try to be perfect, you still make mistakes. Your heart can be perfect, but your performance will never be perfect as long as you are on earth.

You are legally and positionally perfect in Christ, but experientially, you are in the process of changing every day from glory to glory. It is a growing process, and it takes time.

Struggling for perfection to gain acceptance and approval from God or others only brings frustration and never-ending struggle. And it isn't necessary because Jesus accepts you just as you are. He will never pressure you to perform or demand something of you that you don't know how to give. So just do your best . . . and enjoy life while you're maturing.

Your Weakness Is God's Opportunity

My grace (My favor and loving-kindness and mercy)
is enough for you . . . for My strength and power are
made perfect (fulfilled and completed) and show
themselves most effective in [your] weakness.

2 CORINTHIANS 12:9

Do you ever feel hopelessly weak and down on yourself? God wants you to know that the only power weakness has over you is the power you give it.

Disliking yourself because you have weaknesses opens the door to trouble that can affect many areas of your life. But human weakness is no surprise to God. In fact, it is an opportunity for His strength and power to be made perfect in your weakness.

As you meditate on the truth of this promise tonight, make a decision that you will not get so disturbed about your weaknesses that you fail to recognize them as great opportunities for God. Stop grieving over your weaknesses and start receiving God's grace, strength, and power.

Visit the Still Waters

He makes me lie down in [fresh, tender] green
pastures; He leads me beside the still and restful waters.

PSALM 23:2

This particular psalm is familiar to most people, but have you ever given much thought to the "still and restful waters"? I believe this is where you find quiet rest and strength to face the pressures of life.

One might say that the "still waters" are healing waters. The quiet and stillness contain restorative qualities for your soul.

The still waters are available at all times, but we go there far too seldom. Anytime you feel the slightest urge or need you may visit the still waters, if only for a few minutes. Let everything get quiet, and then bask in the beauty of solitude. Silence can teach us more in a moment than all the noise in the world ever could.

So spend more time beside the still waters and find peaceful rest for your soul.

Cooperate with God's Plan

*For I know the thoughts and plans that I have
for you, says the Lord, thoughts and plans for
welfare and peace and not for evil, to give
you hope in your final outcome.*

JEREMIAH 29:11

God has a plan for every person and His Word clearly says it is a good plan. But Satan starts his dirty work early in your life, attempting to pervert and destroy God's good plan. He arranges for all kinds of disappointing, discouraging, hurtful, and frightening events to take place. And often he does a lot of damage.

But no matter how much you have been hurt, God can restore you. If you experienced a bad beginning, do not despair. God is in the business of repair, and His repairs are better than new. However this restoration will not happen automatically. You must believe the Word of God and fully cooperate with Him during the restoration process. Look to Jesus, the One who loves you unconditionally. He is the Author and Finisher of everything in you and your life.

Learn the Power of Patience

For you have need of steadfast patience and en-durance, so that you may perform and fully accom-plish the will of God, and thus receive and carry away [and enjoy to the full] what is promised.

HEBREWS 10:36

Patience is powerful because it frees you from the control of the devil and the cir-cumstances he brings to upset us. However, pa-tience—which is a fruit of the Spirit—only grows through trials. It is during these times that you can develop the ability to remain strong and stable.

Patience is required if you are to see the fulfill-ment of God's promises in your life. So it is impor-tant to develop control over your thoughts and what you say when you are faced with challenging cir-cumstances. It isn't easy, but with God's help you can do it.

Actively pursue the patience of Christ and it will lead you into His power. Then you will be able to accomplish God's will and receive His promises.

Enjoy Kingdom Living

The kingdom of God is not a matter of [getting the] food and drink [one likes], but instead it is righteousness (that state which makes a person acceptable to God) and [heart] peace and joy in the Holy Spirit.

ROMANS 14:17

As a child of God it is your privilege to live in God's kingdom. But what and where is His kingdom? Luke 17:21 says the kingdom of God is within you. And the Scripture for this evening sheds light on what it is and isn't.

The kingdom of God is not food and drink—things of this world—but it is righteousness, peace, and joy in the Holy Spirit. Many people have the wealth of the world, but they do not have true satisfaction.

Satisfaction in your inner man is what Jesus wants to give you. When things are right on the inside, the outward things don't matter as much. So keep your eyes on the true kingdom of God and the rest will be added in abundance.

Exchange Your Guilt for Freedom

Not that I have now attained [this ideal], or have already been made perfect, but I press on to lay hold of (grasp) and make my own, that for which Christ Jesus (the Messiah) has laid hold of me and made me His own.

PHILIPPIANS 3:12

Satan delights in trying to make us feel guilt and condemnation over our past sins and imperfections. I know because I was plagued with these feelings for many years, until God helped me see that I did not need to be perfect to be forgiven. He let me know I was accomplishing nothing beneficial by feeling guilty.

When you repent and turn away from your sin, God does the rest—and He is more than enough. You don't need to add your guilt to His sacrifice. Complete forgiveness is completely free!

Even though you are not perfect, you can accept the forgiveness Jesus says is yours. Exchange your feelings of guilt and condemnation for His unconditional love and find complete and total freedom.

You Can Be Free!

*And all of us . . . are constantly being transfig-
ured into His very own image in ever increasing
splendor and from one degree of glory to another.*

2 CORINTHIANS 3:18

Everyone passes through different levels
of God's glory and obviously we aren't all
at the same level at the same time. Therefore you
hinder the maturing process when you compare
yourself with someone else and then feel as if you
don't measure up. And this is just what the devil
wants.

I call this the performance-acceptance syn-
drome, and if you want to be free you must overcome it. You can do this by seeing yourself through
God's eyes. He sees you as valuable, unique, and
precious, and He loves you just as you are—imperfections and all.

If you are worn out from trying to be perfect,
start enjoying being yourself and trust God to
change you. He knows what He's doing and He will
get the job done if you will just keep on believing.

Be Confident in Christ

[God] Himself has said, I will not in any way fail
you nor give you up nor leave you without
support . . . [I will] not in any degree leave you
helpless nor forsake nor let [you] down (relax My
hold on you)! [Assuredly not!]

HEBREWS 13:5

You are created by a great God for great things. But you will only see the fulfillment of your destiny by placing your confidence in Christ.

Satan works hard attempting to steal your confidence, but you must steadfastly resist him. If you will just remind yourself—and Satan—that it is Jesus who gives you confidence, you can overcome the devil's evil plan.

Don't let insecurities and past failures steal your confidence. God says He will never leave you nor forsake you, so you must believe it and act on it.

Whatever you may be facing right now, remember God is able even when you are not. He loves you and will show himself strong even through your weakness. So just trust and believe.

Stir Up the Gift

That is why I would remind you to stir up (rekindle the embers of, fan the flame of, and keep burning) the [gracious] gift of God, [the inner fire] that is in you.

2 TIMOTHY 1:6

In your spiritual life, you are either aggressively moving forward or slipping backward. Either you grow, or you start to die. There is no such thing as dormant Christianity. It is vital and essential to keep pressing on.

In this passage of Scripture Timothy needed some encouragement. Paul strongly encouraged him to get back on track, remember the call on his life, resist fear, and remember that God had not given him "the spirit of fear; but of power, and of love, and of a sound mind" (2 Timothy 1: 7 KJV). If you find you are feeling stagnant or slipping back into old patterns of thought and behavior, stir up the gift that is within you tonight and press forward in Him.

Character Tests

Oh, let the wickedness of the wicked come to an end, but establish the [uncompromisingly] righteous [those upright and in harmony with You]; for You, Who try the hearts and emotions and thinking powers, are a righteous God.

PSALM 7:9

Have you found yourself wondering lately if the condition of this world can get any worse? Life is filled with challenges that test your determination and your faith in God. Whether faced with the impending threat of terrorism or with simple everyday hassles, the quality of your character is sure to be tested on a regular basis.

You must remember that God tests our hearts, our emotions, and our minds. What does it really mean to test something? Pressure is put on it to see if it will do what it says it will do. Will it hold up under stress? Can it perform at the level its maker says it can? Is it genuine when measured against a true standard of quality? God does the same with us. Ask God to give you grace to pass all your tests.

Fight Doubt and Unbelief

[For Abraham, human reason for] hope being gone,
hoped in faith that he should become the father of
many nations, as he had been promised, so [numberless]
shall your descendants be. . . . No unbelief or distrust
made him waver (doubtingly question) concerning the
promise of God, but he grew strong and was empow-
ered by faith as he gave praise and glory to God.

ROMANS 4:18,20

God had promised Abraham an heir from his own body. Despite his advanced years Abraham was still standing in faith, believing what God had said would come to pass. He kept praising and giving glory to God. As he did so, he grew strong in faith.

It would be ridiculous for God to expect you to do something and not give you the ability to do it. Satan knows how dangerous you are with a heart full of faith, so he attacks you with doubt and unbelief. Keep praising God and give Him glory. Faith will rise in your heart and you will overcome.

Saved from Sin

*For we do not have a High Priest Who is unable to
understand and sympathize and have a shared feeling
with our weaknesses and infirmities and liability to
the assaults of temptation, but One Who has been
tempted in every respect as we are, yet without sin-
ning. Let us then fearlessly and confidently and
boldly draw near to the throne of grace (the
throne of God's unmerited favor to us sinners),
that we may receive mercy [for our failures].*

HEBREWS 4:15-16

Sin is a real issue for most people, but sin
does not have to be a big problem. Do
you know God has already made provision in His
Word for your human failures? Most people make a
much bigger deal out of these things than God does.

Jesus understands your human frailty because
He was tempted in every way we are. Because He is
your High Priest, interceding with the Father for
you, you can come boldly to God's throne to receive
all of His grace, favor, and mercy.

A Willing Heart

And the Lord said to Moses, Speak to the Israelites,
that they take for Me an offering. From every man
who gives it willingly and ungrudgingly with his
heart you shall take My offering.

EXODUS 25:1-2

When we talk about a willing heart, we are basically talking about "want to." Without it we will never do anything.

"Want to" is a powerful thing. With it you can lose weight, keep your house clean, save money, get out of debt, or reach any other goal in life you may have set for yourself. You don't really like to face the fact that your victory or defeat has a lot to do with your "want to."

We like to blame everything on someone or something else. But you need to sit down and take a good old-fashioned inventory of your "want to." You need to be honest enough to say, "Lord, I didn't win the victory because I really didn't want to." Tonight, ask the Lord to give you plenty of "want to."

Satisfy Your Thirst

*I am the Bread of Life. He who comes to Me will
never be hungry, and he who believes in and cleaves
to and trusts in and relies on Me will never
thirst any more (at any time).*

JOHN 6:35

We all thirst for more of God, but if you
don't know He is what you are craving,
you can be easily misled. Instead, if you set your
mind on seeking God—if you give Him first place in
your desires, thoughts, and choices—your thirst will
truly be quenched and you will not be led astray.

David spoke of this longing for the Lord in
Psalm 42:2, saying, "My inner self thirsts for God,
for the living God." You are to search after God like
a thirsty man in the desert. What does a thirsty man
think about? Nothing but water! He isn't concerned
about anything else but finding what it takes to
quench his thirst. Tonight, God is saying to you,
"Here I am, seek Me, I have everything you need."

The Spirit of Holiness

And [as to His divine nature] according to
the Spirit of holiness was openly designated
the Son of God in power.

ROMANS 1:4

The Holy Spirit is the holiness of God and it is His job to work that holiness in all those who believe in Jesus Christ as Savior. 1 Peter 1:15-16 says: "But as the One Who called you is holy, you yourselves also be holy in all your conduct and manner of living. For it is written, You shall be holy, for I am holy."

God would never tell you to be holy without giving you the help you need to make you that way. An unholy spirit could never make you holy. So God sends His Holy Spirit into your heart to do a complete and thorough work. Paul tells you that He who began a good work in you is well able to complete it (see Philippians 1:6). The Spirit of Holiness will continue to work in you as long as you are on this earth; He will continually bring you into new levels of victory.

It Is Finished!

*Therefore, brethren, since we have full freedom and
confidence to enter into the [Holy of] Holies [by the
power and virtue] in the blood of Jesus, by this fresh
(new) and living way which He initiated and dedicated
and opened for us through the separating curtain (veil
of the Holy of Holies), that is, through His flesh, and
since we have [such] a great and wonderful and noble
Priest [Who rules] over the house of God, let us all
come forward and draw near.*

HEBREWS 10:19-22

Before Jesus died on your behalf, the only
way to receive God's promises was by
living a perfect life or by offering a blood sacrifice.
When Jesus died and paid for the sins of mankind
with His own blood, the curtain of the temple
which separated people from the presence of God
was torn in two.

When Jesus spoke from the cross saying, "It is
finished!" He meant that the system of the law was
finished, and now all people can enter freely into the
presence of God. Through the blood of Jesus you
can draw near to God! Ponder this important truth.

Grow in Grace

But grow in grace (undeserved favor, spiritual strength) and recognition and knowledge and understanding of our Lord and Savior Jesus Christ (the Messiah). To Him [be] glory (honor, majesty, and splendor) both now and to the day of eternity. Amen (so be it)!

2 PETER 3:18

Grace is God's power coming into your situation to do for you what you cannot do for yourself. Once you understand grace, you must grow in learning how to receive it in every situation. Trusting God fully is something you grow into—the more you trust Him, the stronger you are spiritually. You only learn to trust God by doing it. You grow in grace by continually putting forth your faith in God and receiving His grace in situations that are difficult or impossible for you.

If you are struggling with something right now in your life, ask yourself honestly if you are putting your faith in God that His grace will meet the need. Tonight, decide to walk in His grace!

Signs of Success

And these attesting signs will accompany those
who believe: in My name they will drive out demons;
they will speak in new languages; they will pick up
serpents; and [even] if they drink anything deadly, it
will not hurt them; they will lay their hands on the
sick, and they will get well.

MARK 16:17-18

Salvation is in the name of Jesus. You are baptized in that name, both in water and the Holy Spirit. You pray and expect your prayers to be heard and answered in that name. The sick are healed and demons are cast out in that wonderful name.

The early disciples used the name of Jesus, and Satan came against them fiercely. The devil does not want you to start anything of value—and if you do manage to get started, he does not want you to finish. He knows well his time on this earth is quickly running out. Accomplish great things in the name of Jesus and finish strong!

Find Your Backbone

*And as for you, brethren, do not become weary or
lose heart in doing right [but continue in
well-doing without weakening].*

2 THESSALONIANS 3:13

Passivity is the opposite of activity. The Word of God clearly teaches that you must be alert, cautious, and active (1 Peter 5:8). The devil knows inactivity will spell the believer's ultimate defeat. As long as you are moving against the devil by using your will to resist him, the enemy will not win the war. However if you enter into a state of passivity, you are in serious trouble.

Passivity can best be described as a lack of desire, general apathy, and laziness. Many believers want the good life but they are passively sitting around "wishing" something good would happen to them. If you desire victory over your problems this evening, if you truly want to live the resurrection life, resolve to have a strong backbone (determination) and not just a wishbone!

The Favorable Time

He who observes the wind [and waits for all con-
ditions to be favorable] will not sow, and he who
regards the clouds will not reap.

ECCLESIASTES 11:4

When the Lord asks His people to do something, there is a temptation to wait for "a convenient season" (Acts 24:25 KJV). There is always the tendency to hold back until it won't be so difficult. The problem is that in order to accomplish something for God, you have to be willing to leave your comfort zone and take on new responsibility.

God expects you to do something that will produce good fruit. If you do not use the gifts and talents that He has given you, then you are not being responsible over what He has entrusted to you. You need to be a person who is unafraid of responsibility and change. It is in times of challenge that you build your strength. If you only do what is easy, you will always remain weak and ineffective. The time to move forward is now!

The Trust Test

*Trust in, lean on, rely on, and have confidence in
Him at all times, you people; pour out your hearts
before Him. God is a refuge for us (a fortress and a
high tower). Selah [pause, and calmly think of that]!*

PSALM 62:8

One thing you can expect to encounter in your journey with God is the trust test. How many times do you say to God, "What is going on in my life? What are You doing? What is happening? I don't understand." If you are in a place right now where nothing in your life makes any sense, trust God anyway.

You are not just to have faith and trust in God once in a while or from time to time, but at all times. You must learn to live from faith to faith, trusting the Lord when things are good and when things are bad. There is no such thing as trusting God without unanswered questions. There are always going to be things you just don't understand.

He Yearns for You

Or do you suppose that the Scripture is speaking
to no purpose that says, The Spirit Whom He has
caused to dwell in us yearns over us and He yearns for
the Spirit [to be welcome] with a jealous love?

JAMES 4:5

According to James 4:4, when you pay more attention to the things of the world than you do to God, He looks upon you as an unfaithful wife who is having an illicit love affair with the world and breaking her marriage vow to Him. To keep you faithful to Him and in close fellowship and communion with Him, sometimes He must remove things from your life that are keeping you from Him.

The Holy Spirit wants to be made welcome; He yearns for fellowship with you. Don't allow jobs, friends, family, money, or success to take His rightful place in your life. Open up your entire life and say with all your heart, "Welcome, Holy Spirit; I am glad You have made Your home in me!"

Holy Ground

And Moses said, I will now turn aside and see this great sight, why the bush is not burned. And when the Lord saw that he turned aside to see, God called to him out of the midst of the bush and said, Moses, Moses! And he said, Here am I. God said, Do not come near; put your shoes off your feet, for the place on which you stand is holy ground.

EXODUS 3:3-5

Moses removed his sandals because he was standing on holy ground. Just moments before, it was ordinary ground—now it was holy. God's presence made it holy!

You are God's tabernacle. Your body is the temple of the Holy Spirit. He lives in you! Wherever you go, He goes. If you go to the grocery store; if you go play golf; if you go to work—He goes. Ordinary things and places are not holy in themselves, but when we go and do them God has promised to be with us. And any place God is becomes holy.

Be of Good Cheer!

*Be strong (confident) and of good courage, for
you shall cause this people to inherit the land
which I swore to their fathers to give them.*

JOSHUA 1:6

In John 16:33, Jesus said, "Be of good
cheer!" One definition of the word *cheer*
in this verse is, "to be of good courage." When the
Lord was giving Joshua direction, He repeatedly
told him to be of good courage. Without the cheerful attitude that God encouraged Joshua to walk in,
he would have given up when the enemy repeatedly
came against him, and the children of Israel would
never have reached the promised land.

The same is true of you in your daily walk. Joy
and cheer give you the strength to carry on toward
the goal the Lord has set before you. Lack of joy is
why many times you give up when you should endure. The presence of courage and a cheerful attitude gives you the endurance to outlast the devil,
overcome your negative circumstances, and "inherit
the land."

The Road of Relationship

If anyone thinks himself to be religious (piously observant of the external duties of his faith) and does not bridle his tongue but deludes his own heart, this person's religious service is worthless (futile, barren).

JAMES 1:26

Sometimes it seems that religion is killing people. There are many who are seeking a relationship with God, but the religious community tells them what they need to "do" in order to be acceptable to Him. This religious spirit was alive in Jesus' day, and even though He died to put an end to it and bring people into close personal relationship with Himself, the Holy Spirit, and the Father, that same spirit still torments people to this day—if they don't know the truth.

Religion says, "You must find a way, no matter how impossible it may seem. You had better follow the rules or suffer punishment." But relationship says, "Do your best because you love Me. I know your heart. Admit your faults, repent of your mistakes, and just keep loving Me."

A Step of Faith

A man's mind plans his way, but the Lord directs
his steps and makes them sure.

PROVERBS 16:9

There are times in life when you must take a step in order to find out, one way or the other, what you should do. Some doors will never open unless you move toward them. At other times you may take a step and find that God will not open the door. If you trust Him for guidance and the door opens easily, you can trust that He is leading you to enter into the opportunity before you.

Sometimes the only way to discover God's will is to practice "stepping out and finding out." If you have prayed about a situation and still don't know what you should do, take a step of faith. We can stand before an automatic door at a supermarket and look at it all day, but it won't open until we step forward to trigger the mechanism. Trust God, take a step, and see if the door opens!

Faint Not

*When you go forth to battle against your enemies
and see horses and chariots and an army greater than
your own, do not be afraid of them, for the Lord your
God, Who brought you out of the land of Egypt, is
with you. . . . Let not your [minds and] hearts faint;
fear not, and do not tremble or be terrified [and
in dread] because of them. For the Lord your
God is He Who goes with you to fight for
you against your enemies to save you.*

DEUTERONOMY 20:1,3-4

A fainthearted person cannot take much.
He has to have everything a certain way
or he gives up and quits. He gets discouraged and
depressed quickly.

What happens when your heart faints? It just
gives up. In your heart you say, "I can't do this. It's
just too hard." If that describes you, know that you
don't have to stay that way. The power of God is
available to you to break that fainthearted spirit off
your life. Instead of thinking and saying, "It is too
hard," say, "I can do whatever I need to do because
God is with me."

Prisoners of Hope

Return to the stronghold [of security and prosperity], you prisoners of hope; even today do I declare that I will restore double your former prosperity to you.

ZECHARIAH 9:12

As a "prisoner of hope," you must be filled with hope, you must think hope, and you must speak hope. Hope is the foundation on which faith stands. Some people try to have faith after having lost all hope. It won't work. Refuse to stop hoping no matter how dry the bones may seem, how dead the situation may appear, or how long the problem has been around.

Psalm 42:5 says, "Why are you cast down, O my inner self? And why should you moan over me and be disquieted within me? Hope in God and wait expectantly for Him, for I shall yet praise Him, my Help and my God." God is still God, and if you will remain positive and become a "prisoner of hope," He will restore to you double everything you have lost.

A Word in Season

*[The Servant of God says] The Lord God has
given Me the tongue of a disciple and of one
who is taught, that I should know how to speak a
word in season to him who is weary. He wakens Me
morning by morning, He wakens My ear to hear
as a disciple [as one who is taught].*

ISAIAH 50:4

You can bless people with the words of your mouth. The power of life and death is in the tongue (see Proverbs 18:21), therefore you can speak life to others. Proverbs 15:23 says, "A man has joy in making an apt answer, and a word spoken at the right moment—how good it is!" When you edify or exhort, you are urging people forward in Christ. You can actually hold people back or encourage them forward just by your words.

What a tremendous honor to be used by God to lift up another. Ask Him to teach you; to give you words in season that will heal and encourage, bless and edify.

No Fear

For God did not give us a spirit of timidity (of cowardice, of craven and cringing and fawning fear), but [He has given us a spirit] of power and of love and of calm and well-balanced mind and discipline and self-control.

2 TIMOTHY 1:7

In this passage of Scripture, Paul was encouraging Timothy and saying, "You may feel like giving up, but you have everything you need to succeed. The Holy Spirit gives you peace and the power to face anything. Press on without fear!"

You may not understand what is going on in the world around you, but you must trust God through it all. You can pray and ask God for answers, but when heaven is silent you need to keep doing what God has told us to do and just trust Him. God will make all the pieces work together for His purpose, even when you don't see tomorrow clearly. Tomorrow's answers usually don't come until tomorrow.

Not of This World

*Do not be conformed to this world (this age),
[fashioned after and adapted to its external, superficial customs], but be transformed (changed) by the
[entire] renewal of your mind [by its new ideals and
its new attitude], so that you may prove [for your-
selves] what is the good and acceptable and perfect
will of God, even the thing which is good and
acceptable and perfect [in His sight for you].*

ROMANS 12:2

Constant vigilance is required to avoid
becoming like the world. You are ex-
posed to so much violence today that you hardly notice it or pay any attention to it. Many people are
desensitized to the agonies real people suffer due to
the wealth of violence that is seen in movies and on
television.

You may reach the point where you have no em-
pathy for people that are suffering. This is under-
standable, but not acceptable. You must fight apathy.
As a Christian, you may not be able to solve all the
world's problems, but you can care—and to truly
end this day right, you can pray.

Crowned with Favor

You have made him but a little lower than God [or heavenly beings], and You have crowned him with glory and honor. You made him to have dominion over the works of Your hands; You have put all things under his feet.

PSALM 8:5-6

In this Scripture, honor and favor have the same meaning. According to this promise you can have favor with God and with other people. But just because something is available to you does not mean you will partake of it. The Lord offers many gifts that you never receive and enjoy because you don't activate your faith in that area.

For example, if you go to a job interview confessing fear and failure, you will be almost certain not to get the job. On the other hand, even if you apply for a job you aren't fully qualified for, you can still go in confidence, knowing God will give you favor in every situation that is His will.

In His Time

Nevertheless, do not let this one fact escape you,
beloved, that with the Lord one day is as a thousand
years and a thousand years as one day.

2 PETER 3:8

God moves in His timing, not yours. He is never late, but He is usually not early either. He is often the God of the midnight hour. He sometimes waits until the last second before He gives you what you need. Before He intervenes on your behalf, He has to be sure you are not going to take matters into your own hands and do something out of His perfect timing.

You must learn to trust God's timing. But first your self-will and your spirit of independence must be broken so that God is free to work His will in your life and circumstances. If you are waiting for something, set aside your own timetable tonight. Trust God and believe that while you are waiting for your breakthrough, He is doing a good work in you for His purpose.

Submit to Authority

Be submissive to every human institution and authority for the sake of the Lord, whether it be to the emperor as supreme, or to governors as sent by him to bring vengeance (punishment, justice) to those who do wrong and to encourage those who do good service.

I PETER 2:13-14

A godly response to those in authority over you provides you with spiritual safety. If you submit to authority for the sake of honoring God and His Word, you will enjoy a free flow of His anointing in your life. If you rebel and refuse to submit, you will block the anointing. Submission protects you from demonic attack, while rebellion opens the door for the enemy.

Live by the anointing. God has given it to you to help you in all that you do. You must remember that things are accomplished by the Spirit of God and not by might nor by power (see Zechariah 4:6). Tonight, stay peaceful and calm; be quick to forgive, slow to anger, patient, and kind. You'll find that your anointing will be stronger.

The Apple of His Eye

The Lord makes poor and makes rich;
He brings low and He lifts up.

1 SAMUEL 2:7

A perfect example of this Scripture is found in the life of Esther. God raised her up out of obscurity to become the queen of the entire land. He gave her favor with everyone she met, including the king. Esther drew upon that favor to save herself and her people from being murdered by the evil Haman. Despite great personal risk, she was not afraid to go to the king and ask him to intervene, because she had favor with God.

Regardless what circumstances come into your life, believe God for supernatural favor. Despite how hopeless things may seem, God can lift you up. If your life is in His hands, the light of the Lord shines upon you. It is time you believe the words of your Father: "You are the apple of My eye. You are My child." Think about that as you end your day right!

A Kind Reward

*But love your enemies and be kind and do good
[doing favors so that someone derives benefit from
them] and lend, expecting and hoping for nothing in
return but considering nothing as lost and despairing
of no one; and then your recompense (your reward)
will be great (rich, strong, intense, and abundant).*

LUKE 6:35

Has God ever asked you to do something really special for somebody who hurt you? If so, I am sure that like me you found it very difficult to do. Perhaps you have spent a lot of time in your life blessing someone who never blesses you in return. In that case, don't become bitter but trust God to reward you.

Some of us are a little more naturally disposed toward kindness than others. Many of us find we can be kind to those who are kind to us, but we run into trouble with those we don't think deserve kindness. God delights in being kind to those of us who don't deserve it. Actually, kindness isn't even kindness unless it is extended toward the undeserving.

End your day by being kind to someone.

Once and For All

He went once for all into the [Holy of] Holies [of heaven], not by virtue of the blood of goats and calves [by which to make reconciliation between God and man], but His own blood, having found and secured a complete redemption (an everlasting release for us).

HEBERWS 9:12

Under the Old Covenant, the sins of the people were covered, but they were never rid of the consciousness of sin. The blood of bulls and goats could be used for the purification of the body, but it could never reach the inner man and purify his conscience (see Hebrews 10:1-3).

Everything until that time was done to "tide us over," until the fullness of God's time. But when the time came to put into action the plan God had announced in the Garden of Eden, He sent His Son to do the job right. Jesus offered His blood once and for all. This means two things—first, He never has to do it again, and second; it has been done for everyone. You can go to sleep tonight knowing your sins are completely forgiven.

Freedom and Liberty

Now the Lord is the Spirit, and where the Spirit
of the Lord is, there is liberty (emancipation
from bondage, freedom).

2 CORINTHIANS 3:17

Jesus came to set the captives free. You are not free to do whatever you feel like doing, but you have been set free from legalism and are now free to follow the leadership of the Holy Spirit. A legalistic mentality says that everybody has to do exactly the same thing, the same way, all the time. But realize tonight the Spirit of God leads us individually, and often in unique, creative ways.

Jesus wants you to have liberty and not legalism. If the Son has set you free, you are free indeed (see John 8:36). You are free from sin. Free from manipulation and control. Free from competition with others. Free from addiction. Free from fear. Free from selfishness. Free to be who you are. Free! Free! Free!

Turn Away from Evil

Turn not to those [mediums] who have familiar spirits or to wizards; do not seek them out to be defiled by them. I am the Lord your God.

LEVITICUS 19:31

This is a serious command! Spiritualism, divination, and witchcraft are all forbidden in the Word of God. Many people, including some who consider themselves to be Christians, participate in practices that God considers vile and evil. God says He will set His face against anyone who turns to mediums and spiritists to prostitute themselves by following them (see Leviticus 20:6). Yet Christians still read horoscopes and consult psychics and wonder why they don't have peace.

God wants you to seek Him and it offends Him if you seek these other sources. No one who does so will ever have a peaceful, joy-filled, and prosperous life. If you have been involved in any activity of this sort, I strongly encourage you to thoroughly repent, ask God to forgive you, and turn away completely from such practices.

Give Thanks Every Day

In everything give thanks; for this is the will of
God in Christ Jesus for you.

I THESSALONIANS 5:18 NKJV

During this Thanksgiving month, I encourage you to take time each day to
thank God for something He has done for you. You
are to thank Him always for everything—great or
small—but being specific about something each day
that is especially meaningful to you will be a blessing
to you . . . and to God.

There is so much in life to be thankful for, and
that's where you need to keep your focus—not just
on Thanksgiving Day but every day.

Fill your mind with memories that are true,
pure, lovely, excellent, and worthy of praise. Then
express your thanks to God. As the psalmist says in
Psalm 100:4, "Be thankful and say so to Him, bless
and affectionately praise His name!" End this day
right by being thankful.

Cherish the Anointing

*But as for you, the anointing (the sacred appoint-
ment, the unction) which you received from Him
abides [permanently] in you; [so] then . . . you must
abide in (live in, never depart from) Him.*

1 JOHN 2:27

You have a precious treasure within you
as a believer in Christ. The presence and
power of the Holy Spirit dwells in you through the
anointing. You can depend on it to lead and instruct
you.

The anointing makes such a difference in your
daily living. Without it everything is a struggle. But
with the anointing, all things are possible. Only as
you understand the anointing can you know how to
release it and increase it in your life.

You are empowered by the anointing for service
and fruitfulness. So learn to respect it, be thankful
for it, and put it to good use. Let it flow first to you
to minister to your needs. Then let it flow through
you to make a meaningful difference in the lives of
those around you.

Seek to Be Humble

Do nothing from factional motives [through contentiousness, strife, selfishness, or for unworthy ends] or prompted by conceit and empty arrogance. Instead, in the true spirit of humility (lowliness of mind) let each regard the others as better than and superior to himself.

PHILIPPIANS 2:3

Having pure motives and humility are required if you are to fulfill the command to think more highly of others than yourself. In fact it cannot happen without a willingness to be obedient to the Holy Spirit.

To live in harmony you must recognize and respect the right of others to disagree with you, and you must do so with a good attitude. Humility requires that you forgive quickly and frequently . . . and that you not be easily offended. You cannot be self seeking, but instead you must be generous in mercy and patience.

Humble yourself and follow God's instructions and you will enjoy the wonderful benefits of obedience: peace, joy, and a powerful, victorious life.

Pray with Boldness and Confidence

Let us then fearlessly and confidently and boldly draw near to the throne of grace . . . that we may receive mercy . . . and find grace to help in good time for every need [appropriate help and well-timed help, coming just when we need it].

HEBREWS 4:16

Prayer opens the windows of heaven and touches the heart of God. It is a beautiful and powerful privilege that brings many changes in both circumstances and people. Prayer is often the difference between confusion and clarity, hurt and healing, defeat and victory, and even between life and death.

There are many ways to pray, but the best way is to pray boldly and effectually. God loves you and He doesn't want your communication with Him to be vague and unclear. He wants you to come to Him fearlessly and confidently, being specific in your prayers.

Exercise the liberty and privilege of prayer tonight, fully expecting to receive the promised help just when you need it.

The Son Has Set You Free

So if the Son liberates you [makes you free men],
then you are really and unquestionably free.

JOHN 8:36

Are you "really and unquestionably free"? If you allow yourself to be controlled by other people, thoughts, feelings, and habits, you are not free.

People who are free are spontaneous and unconfined, not bound, fastened, or attached. They are not limited by past mistakes because they serve a God to whom nothing is impossible.

The psalmist made this bold statement in Psalm 119:45: "I will walk at liberty and at ease." By saying "I will," he indicates he has made a decision to be free and refuses to be in bondage.

I believe this is what God wants you to do. He wants you to have enough holy boldness to declare that the Son has liberated you from all bondage and that you are determined to walk in the glorious freedom He has provided for you.

Experience God's Peace and Rest

The Lord . . . has given peace and
rest to His people.
I CHRONICLES 23:25

This declaration of David speaks of a God who has faithfully given peace and rest to His people—down through the ages, and still today.

In your busy world, your days are often filled to overflowing with all kinds of work and activities that can drain you of your physical energy and leave your mind reeling from the sheer volume.

I'm sure it was the same in David's day. The pace may have been slower but the responsibilities were just as demanding and draining. But David knew the secret to receiving the goodness of God was thanking and praising the Lord both morning and evening.

If you feel drained from a trying day, spend some quiet time with the Lord before you go to bed. Tell Him how much you thank Him and praise Him for being with you today . . . and for the peace and rest you are about to experience as you lie down to sleep.

Abide in the Vine

I am the Vine; you are the branches. Whoever
lives in Me and I in him bears much (abundant)
fruit. However, apart from Me [cut off from
vital union with Me] you can do nothing.

JOHN 15:5

In God's order of things, right thinking comes first and right actions follow. I believe that correct behavior is a "fruit" of right thinking. Many believers struggle, trying to do right, but fruit is not the product of struggling. Fruit comes as a result of abiding in the Vine.

As a Spirit-filled Christian, you are to manifest the fruit of His Spirit, things like kindness, gentleness, meekness, and humility. You are created in His image and you can have the same soothing countenance Jesus displayed. Your words can bring encouragement, edification, and exhortation, which are produced by a pure and positive mind.

As you abide in the Vine, seek to bear much good fruit and exhibit His image and nature. Your own life will be richly blessed and you will be a blessing to others.

Speak a Blessing into Your Life

*He who invokes a blessing on himself . . . shall do
so by saying, May the God of truth and fidelity . . .
bless me; and he . . . shall swear by the God of truth
and faithfulness to His promises . . . because the
former troubles are forgotten and because
they are hidden from My eyes.*

ISAIAH 65:16

You can bless or curse yourself with your mouth. You can bring a blessing by speaking positive truths from God's Word . . . or you can bring a curse by speaking negatively.

Satan is a deceiver and He tries to bring you trouble and then influence you to prophesy that same kind of trouble for your future. But you can choose to bless yourself. If you mentally stop living in the past you can begin to think and speak in agreement with God.

Take notice of the things you say, because what you say does matter—to you and to your well-being. Say what you believe Jesus would say in your situation, and you will open the door for the miracle-working power of God.

Live the Good Life

*For we are . . . recreated in Christ Jesus, [born
anew] that we may do those good works which God
predestined (planned beforehand) for us [taking paths
which He prepared ahead of time], that we should
walk in them [living the good life which He
prearranged and made ready for us to live].*

EPHESIANS 2:10

The heart of God is a father's heart and
He wants you to take full advantage of
the good life that He prearranged for you. Yet many
Christians settle for less than God's best for their
lives because they listen to the devil's lies.

The devil tries to convince you that you've made
too many serious mistakes in the past and disobeyed
God too many times to live the good life. But this is
not true.

We all make mistakes, but God still loves us, and
when you repent He is quick to forgive you and lead
you back to the right path.

God has provided the best . . . and you might as
well have it!

Bend Before You Break

Readily adjust yourself to [people, things]
and . . . if possible, as far as it depends
on you, live at peace with everyone.

ROMANS 12:16,18

You live in a fast-paced world that seems to be placing more demands on you with each passing year. People are hurrying everywhere, and often they are rude and short-tempered. It seems the very atmosphere of the world is charged with stress and pressure.

But the good news is that as a Christian, you don't have to operate on the world's system, reacting like the world. The world responds to difficulties by getting upset, but Jesus said in John 14:27 that you should stop allowing yourself to be agitated, disturbed, and upset.

You do this by learning to be adaptable. It's not always easy on the flesh to give in and do things differently, but it is easier than being upset and miserable.

Learn to bend so you won't break. Allow God's Spirit to lead you out of a stressful lifestyle into one of peace and joy.

Practical Ways for Your Days

Oh, that they had such a [mind and] heart in them always [reverently] to fear Me and keep all My commandments, that it might go well with them and with their children forever!

DEUTERONOMY 5:29

God's Word offers wise instructions about how to make the practice of peace a part of your everyday life.

First of all, you need to hush. Be still and stop all the rushing around. "Be still, and know that I am God" (Psalm 46:10 KJV). The creator of the universe wants a word with you, but how can He really talk to you if you're always on the go? Chill . . . and listen!

Second, you must prepare your heart to receive Him and to hear His voice on a regular basis. This requires a reverent fear of God and obedience to His commandments.

Finally, you must acknowledge Him in everything you do. Make it a lifestyle to be identified with Jesus Christ and faithfully be a doer of the Word. The rewards are great!

Be Fruitful for God

We . . . have not ceased to pray and make [special]
request for you, [asking] that you may . . . walk (live
and conduct yourselves) in a manner worthy
of the Lord, fully pleasing to Him . . .
bearing fruit in every good work.

COLOSSIANS 1:9-10

We live in a busy world . . . and most of us are far too busy. God never told you to be busy, but He says a lot in His Word about being fruitful. One of His first instructions to Adam and Eve was to be fruitful and multiply. And Genesis 8:17 records the same commandment to Noah. To multiply means to "increase."

God wants you to increase by working with what you have. He supplies you with many seeds—gifts and talents—but you must cultivate and use them.

God has planted some great things in you, and as you water and nourish what He has planted, He will give the increase. So work with Him. You are a special person, uniquely called to bear fruit as only you can do.

Overcome Evil with Good

Do not let yourself be overcome by evil, but overcome (master) evil with good.

ROMANS 12:21

As a Christian, you can resist the enemy and overcome evil by having an aggressive, power-packed attitude. You can release positive spiritual power that will always conquer negative power. But it doesn't happen automatically. You must take a spiritually aggressive position and stand your ground.

Dealing with people requires a different approach, however. You are to treat people with dignity, respect, and love. For myself, I had to learn how to be a "lion-hearted lamb"—spiritually strong in dealing with the enemy and meek and gentle in dealing with people.

Being good to people will require that you walk in love, which is an effort that always costs you something. But people who are spiritually powerful always walk in love. It is God's way of overcoming evil with good. And it is well worth the effort.

Be a Good Example

Teach what is fitting and becoming to sound (wholesome) doctrine [the character and right living that identify true Christians].

TITUS 2:1

Being a Christian is not so much a matter of doing as it is of being. When you're willing to get out there and shine, you'll eventually swallow up the darkness in your realm of influence.

God anoints normal, everyday people to live supernaturally in a frustrating world. He wants you to be a doer of the Word and not a hearer only. He wants you to stop just telling people Jesus loves them and start letting Jesus flow through you to meet their needs.

The best way to show the love of Christ is by example. People in the world want to see Christians who live what they preach and teach.

You can be a shining *example* of a victorious Christian, and that's the best way to "teach what it fitting."

Enjoy Life Like a Child

Unless you repent (change, turn about) and become like little children [trusting, lowly, loving, forgiving], you can never enter the kingdom of heaven.

MATTHEW 18:3

As a believer you can have the abundant quality of life that comes from God. He is not impatient or in a hurry. He takes time to enjoy His creation, the works of His hands. And He wants you to do the same.

Joy is available to you if you know how to tap into it. I have learned that simplicity brings joy and complication blocks it. Instead of getting entangled with the complications of religion, you must return to the simplicity of believing and maintaining a Father/child relationship.

God wants you to approach life with childlike faith. He wants you to grow up in your behavior but remain childlike in your attitude of trust and dependence on Him.

Living your life with the simplicity of a child will change your whole outlook in a most amazing way.

You Can Be Molded into His Image

For those whom He foreknew . . . He also destined
from the beginning . . . to be molded into the image
of His Son [and share inwardly His likeness].

ROMANS 8:29

Your goal as a Christian is to become Christlike. The Bible says you are an ambassador of Christ and that He personally makes His appeal to the world through you. The only way you can ever properly represent Jesus to the world is to let His character show through your attitudes and actions. This can only happen through divine transformation, and that's exactly what God had in mind from the beginning of time.

God predestined you to be molded into His image. He said, "Behold, as the clay is in the potter's hand, so are you in My hand" (Jeremiah 18:6). In your relationship with God, you are the clay and He is the potter, and you must never forget that. Become pliable in the Master Potter's hands as He molds you into a vessel He can use to change many lives.

Let Go of All Anger

When angry, do not sin; do not ever let your wrath
(your exasperation, your fury or indignation) last
until the sun goes down. Leave no [such] room or
foothold for the devil [give no opportunity to him].

EPHESIANS 4:26-27

Everyone has anger from time to time, and understanding it and knowing how to handle it properly is important.

Anger begins as a feeling and then manifests itself in words and actions. You feel something, and it causes you to do or say something. Anger is not necessarily always sin—however, what you choose to do with anger directly determines your quality of life.

All anger has the same effect on your life. It upsets you, causing you to feel pressure. Keeping anger locked inside can even be dangerous to your health. So you must take responsibility for your anger and learn to deal with it.

If you struggle with anger, ask God to help you process it and bring it to closure. You can be bitter or better—the choice is yours!

Discover the Cure for the Insecure

May Christ through your faith [actually] dwell
(settle down, abide, make His permanent home)
in your hearts! May you be rooted deep in
love and founded securely on love.

EPHESIANS 3:17

The world is full of insecure people. In fact an article I once read described insecurity as a psychological disturbance of epidemic proportions. So is there a cure for the insecure?

The answer is yes. The Word of God says that you can be secure through Jesus Christ. As a believer, you will find our Lord Jesus Christ is the only lasting cure for insecurity. He took all of your insecurities upon himself at Calvary. His death and resurrection purchased your freedom from the pain and behavior patterns produced by a lifetime of insecurity.

All the areas of your life that are out of order can be reconciled through Jesus and the work He accomplished on the cross. Start believing it—and remember: "The Lord your God is with you wherever you go" (Joshua 1:9).

Receive the Goodness of God

*Whatever is good and perfect comes to us from
God above, who created all heaven's lights. Unlike
them, he never changes or casts shifting shadows.*

JAMES 1:17 NLT

There was a time when I believed God was good—but I wasn't sure He would be good to *me*. I was afraid I hadn't been good enough to receive His goodness. But He taught me that our inability to do everything right doesn't cancel out His goodness. Thankfully, receiving God's goodness is based on His righteousness, not ours.

I now keep a journal to list all the good things God does for me. This gives me a greater appreciation for His provisions and confirms His constant flow of blessings in my life.

God is good, and His goodness radiates from Him like heat radiates from the sun. And those rays of goodness reach out to you every day. Make a list of all His blessings, and you'll have no doubt about the good and perfect gifts that come from Him.

Exercise Moderation

I discipline my body . . . training it
to do what it should.

1 CORINTHIANS 9:27 NLT

The holidays are upon us again! From the traditional American observation of Thanksgiving and the celebration of our Savior's birth to the first day of the brand-new year, the holidays present us with ample opportunities to celebrate . . . and to eat.

For many who tend to overeat and gain weight, it can be a challenging time. But it doesn't have to be that way. With God's help you can discipline yourself instead of giving in to all your food desires.

I'm not suggesting you stay away from the Thanksgiving dinner, the Christmas Brunch, or the New Year's gathering. It's not necessary to sacrifice all your seasonal favorites, but it is important to exercise moderation. Pray and ask God to help you focus on the season instead of the food . . . and receive a double blessing.

Give Thanks with a Grateful Heart

Bless (affectionately, gratefully praise) the Lord, O my soul, and forget not [one of] all His benefits.

PSALM 103:2

In a few days you will be celebrating a day set aside to give thanks to God for all His blessings. You are probably already making plans and preparations for this special day. As you prepare, begin to think about all the wonderful things God has given you this year.

It might be a good idea to make a list. You won't be able to think of all your blessings, but you will remember enough to humble you and fill you with gratitude.

Then on Thanksgiving Day don't allow the activities that are attached to the traditions of Thanksgiving to crowd out the real purpose of the day. Talk about the goodness of God and share about one or two special blessings.

Don't forget to thank God for life, family, friends, and provisions. Most important, express your special thanks to Him.

Get Ready for the Joy

Weeping may endure for a night, but joy comes in the morning.

PSALM 30:5

Does your happiness depend on everything in your life being just right? If you think you can't be happy until all your circumstances are right, you will never be happy. We all experience times in life when we feel down for various reasons, but you can't allow your circumstances to control your emotions.

Satan seeks to fill your mind with negative thoughts and emotions that cause you to feel down because He is a discourager. But Jesus is your encourager and He came to lift you up. He came to give you righteousness, joy, and all the things that cause you to feel "up"!

We all experience times of frustration and distress over unfulfilled hopes and dreams. When things don't go according to your plans, it's normal to feel disappointment. Things may make you feel sad temporarily, but when you know that weeping only lasts for a time and then comes joy, it makes everything better.

Be Happy

Blessed (happy, fortunate, to be envied) is he who has forgiveness of his transgression continually exercised upon him, whose sin is covered. Blessed (happy, fortunate, to be envied) is the man to whom the Lord imputes no iniquity and in whose spirit there is no deceit.

PSALM 32:1-2

God created you to live the abundant life He died to provide for you—and knowing your sins are completely forgiven should be enough to keep you happy.

But many Christians operate in the works of the flesh trying to serve God. They spend so much time trying to be good they miss the blessing of simple prayer and fellowship with God.

God is not seeking your "works." He wants you! You must remind yourself that you have been made righteous through the death and resurrection of Jesus . . . and you can add nothing to that.

As a Christian, you are no longer your own— you were purchased by the blood of Jesus. He paid the ultimate price for your happiness, so enjoy it.

Trust the Unchanging Rock

Jesus Christ (the Messiah) is [always] the same,
yesterday, today, [yes] and forever.

HEBREWS 13:8

Feelings are emotions that are always changing, so you cannot depend on them. As a follower of Christ, you must learn to live by truth and wisdom, not by feelings and emotions.

1 Corinthians 10:4 refers to Jesus as the Rock. An important part of His nature is His emotional maturity, which includes unchanging stability. During His time on earth, Jesus did not allow himself to be led around by His emotions. He was led by the Spirit even though He was subject to all the same feelings we experience in our daily lives. Jesus was always the same.

And He is still the same . . . and will be forever. You can safely put your trust in Him tonight, knowing He will not change, but will help you develop the same kind of emotional maturity and stability that marked His own life.

Make Excellence a Habit

The righteous man walks in his integrity.

PROVERBS 20:7

Integrity is defined as "a firm adherence to a code or standard of values; soundness." As a Christian, your standards should be much higher than those of the world. What would an integrity check reveal about you? It's something to think about.

People of integrity are committed to a life of excellence—seeking to be better or to go beyond what is normally expected of them. Having integrity means you do the right thing even when nobody is looking . . . and you keep your word even if it costs you something.

I encourage you to make excellence a habit, by following the example of Jesus, our standard of integrity. As God's representative, you are called to show the world what He is like—and you may be the only Bible some people read.

Seek God's Wisdom

If any of you is deficient in wisdom, let him ask of
the giving God [Who gives] to everyone liberally
and ungrudgingly, without reproaching or
faultfinding, and it will be given him.

JAMES 1:5

If things seem so complicated that you're no longer able to enjoy life as God intended, it's time to seek God's wisdom. In all things, God wants you to acknowledge and seek Him, use wisdom, and make the best decisions you know how to make.

Through a simple prayer from wherever you are, you can ask God for wisdom about any situation you face. Before you commit to participating in certain activities, buying things, or being involved with other people, check with God. If you have peace about it, then proceed. But if you don't feel right about it, wait.

Seek God's wisdom and make decisions based on what you sense in your spirit. Then move forward, believing that God will bless you because you acknowledge Him in your decisions.

Listen for God's Voice

My sheep hear My voice, and I know
them, and they follow me.

JOHN 10:27 NKJV

One of the questions that people most frequently ask me is "How can I know specifically what God wants me to do?"

Of all the ways God speaks to you, He most frequently uses peace, wisdom, and the voice of our conscience—that still, small voice inside your spirit that tells you what is right and wrong. The Holy Spirit, who dwells in believers, speaks to your spirit what He wants you to do. Your spirit then communicates the message to your mind, and your mind is then enlightened on what action to take.

God is speaking to you! And He wants to direct you in every area of your life. So delight yourself in Him, follow after peace, and obey the voice of your conscience.

You Reap What You Sow

Whatsoever a man soweth, that shall he also reap.

GALATIANS 6:7 KJV

As God's representative here on earth, your purpose is to do right and glorify God. When you do right, you bring God glory by manifesting His excellence in a tangible way.

One way you can bring Him glory is in the way you treat people. There are many practical ways you can be a blessing to others. You can build others up by giving them a compliment. You can express your appreciation and acknowledge people by giving them a pat on the back or writing them a note of encouragement.

You can also take advantage of opportunities to listen to people and lend a helping hand when they need it. You can believe the best of others and offer forgiveness to those who have offended you.

I encourage you to treat everybody with love and respect. You will not only glorify God, you will also receive blessings by reaping what you sow.

Develop the Mind of the Spirit

The mind of the flesh . . . [is sense and reason without the Holy Spirit] . . . but the mind of the [Holy] Spirit is life and [soul] peace.

ROMANS 8:6

As a young Christian I was always trying to figure out the "why" behind everything and planning excessively for what was ahead. But one day God required me to give it up. He showed me that reasoning is the opposite of trust.

The Bible tells us that the mind of the flesh is sense and reason without the Holy Spirit. It is being hostile to God and refusing to submit to His ways. But the mind of the Spirit is life and soul peace.

If you want to be free of trying to figure everything out, you can develop the mind of the Spirit by constantly renewing your mind with the Word. Little by little, the Word will wash away the wrong thinking and replace it with truth . . . follow that truth instead of your own ability to reason things out and you'll have new life and peace.

Get Away with God

*Are you tired? Worn out? Burned out on religion?
Come to me. Get away with me and you'll recover
your life. I'll show you how to take a real rest. Walk
with me and work with me—watch how I do it.
Learn the unforced rhythms of grace. I won't lay
anything heavy or ill-fitting on you. Keep company
with me and you'll learn to live freely and lightly.*

MATTHEW 11:28-30 THE MESSAGE

That sounds good, doesn't it? I've had enough "heavy stuff" in my life, and I want to enjoy freedom. When you are overloaded with the cares of life you need some help. Your mind needs rest from worrying, your emotions need rest from being upset, and your will needs a rest from stubbornness and rebellion. So you need to be humble enough to call out to God and say, "I need help!"

Your beginning doesn't have to dictate your ending. Get God involved in every area of your life and allow Him to lead you into "real rest."

Still the Storm

> *And He arose and rebuked the wind and said to*
> *the sea, Hush now! Be still (muzzled)! And the*
> *wind ceased (sank to rest as if exhausted by*
> *its beating) and there was [immediately] a*
> *great calm (a perfect peacefulness).*
>
> MARK 4:39

When Jesus and the disciples were crossing the lake and a storm arose, the disciples panicked. They were as stormy inside as the tempest around them. But when Jesus spoke "Peace, be still" out of that well of peace within Him, immediately the wind and the waves became calm.

You cannot rebuke the storms in your life if you have a storm raging on the inside of you. We maintain peace by trusting God. Don't be mad at God because you didn't get what you prayed for. Don't be mad at God because your friend got a promotion at work and you didn't. Don't be mad at God because your friend got married and you're still single. Trusting God in every situation is the only way to still the storm within.

Dreams and Visions

Where there is no vision [no redemptive revelation of God], the people perish.

PROVERBS 29:18

The Israelites had no positive vision for their lives—no dreams. They knew where they came from, but they did not know where they were going. Everything was based on what they had already seen and could see. They did not know how to see with "the eye of faith."

Jesus came to open the prison doors and set the captives free. You will only begin to progress when you start to believe you can experience freedom. You must have a positive vision for your life—a vision for a future that is not determined by your past or even your present circumstances.

Exercise your faith tonight and take a positive look at the possibilities God has planned for you. Begin to "call those things that be not as though they are" (see Romans 4:17). Think and speak about your future in a positive way, according to what God has placed in your heart.

An Inheritance of Peace

Peace I leave with you; My [own] peace I now give and bequeath to you. Not as the world gives do I give to you. Do not let your hearts be troubled, neither let them be afraid.

JOHN 14:27

The word *bequeath* in this verse is a term used in the execution of wills. In preparation for death, people usually bequeath their possessions, especially those things of value, as a blessing to those they love who are left behind.

Jesus knew He was about to pass from this world and He wanted to leave us something. He could have left any number of good things, like His power and His name, and He did. But He also left us His peace.

You don't leave junk for people you love—you leave them the best you have. Jesus had a special kind of peace that surpassed anything mankind had ever known. He knew it was one of the most precious things He could give. Ask for and receive your inheritance tonight!

A Calm Delight

You will show me the path of life; in
Your presence is fullness of joy.

PSALM 16:11

When you consider joy, you may imme-diately think about one of those bubbly people you know who is "up" all of the time, and perhaps you are not like that. I'm not like that ei-ther. But for those of us who tend to be more seri-ous, it is important that we also learn how to have fun, to cut loose, and lighten up a little.

What is joy and what is joy based on? *Joy* is de-fined as "a shout; a proclamation that can manifest in singing; a calm delight." Your joy is not to be based on your circumstances. Happiness may be based on what is happening to you, but not joy. Joy—a fruit of the Spirit—is like a deep well on the inside of you. It is not the fruit of your circumstance. No matter what you are facing in life, you can have joy in the midst of it. Learn to abide in the midst of a calm delight.

His Words

But the Lord said to me, Say not, I am only a
youth; for you shall go to all to whom I shall send
you, and whatever I command you, you shall speak.
Be not afraid of them [their faces], for I am with you
to deliver you, says the Lord. Then the Lord put forth
His hand and touched my mouth. And the Lord said
to me, Behold, I have put My words in your mouth.

JEREMIAH 1:7-9

God called Jeremiah as "a prophet to the nations," and He had to straighten out Jeremiah's mouth before He could use him.

It is no different with you. You must understand that when God calls you to do something, you should not say you cannot do it. If God says you can, then you can! So often we speak out of our insecurities, or we verbalize what others have said about us, or what the devil has told us. Make a decision tonight that from now on you will say about yourself what God says about you.

A Deeper Walk

*When He had stopped speaking, He said to Simon
(Peter), Put out into the deep [water], and
lower your nets for a haul.*

LUKE 5:4

Faith is deposited in the spirit. Romans
12:3 says that every man is given a measure of faith. Faith is a force that comes out of the
spirit, and it can accomplish great things, but faith
must be released to be of value.

If you have faith in your heart to step out and do
something but begin to take counsel with your
mind, negative, doubtful, and unbelieving thoughts
can talk you right out of what faith is telling you. If
your head believes the opposite of what your spirit
is telling you, you must go deeper.

Do you want a haul of blessings in your life? If
the answer is yes, then like the disciples, you have to
leave the shallow places of your own soul—what
you think and feel—for the deeper life in God . . .
what you know down deep inside.

By His Spirit

Not by might, nor by power, but by My Spirit [of Whom the oil is a symbol], says the Lord of hosts.

ZECHARIAH 4:6

It is only by the power of the Holy Spirit living inside you that you can have true success in life. In your own strength you simply become tired and frustrated. But allowing the Holy Spirit to work through you brings contentment and deep joy to your life. You need to give your problems to God and spend your time doing something for those around you who are hurting. Through the anointing of the Holy Spirit, you can do anything.

Real joy comes from being an empty vessel for God's use and glory. At the close of this day, let Him choose where He's going to take you, what He's going to do with you, and when He's going to do it—without arguing about it. It's one thing to be willing to do *everything* for the glory of God (1 Corinthians 10:31); it's another thing entirely to be willing to do *anything* for Him.

Exercise Self-Control

And in [exercising] knowledge [develop] self-control, and in [exercising] self-control [develop] steadfastness (patience, endurance), and in [exercising] steadfastness [develop] godliness [piety].

2 PETER 1:6

Jesus not only commanded you to not allow your heart to be troubled and afraid, He also said, "[Stop allowing yourselves to be agitated and disturbed; and do not permit yourselves to be fearful and intimidated and cowardly and unsettled]" (John 14:27).

You can choose not to get upset. If you are around someone whose good opinion you value, it's amazing how much easier it can be to control yourself. It's much harder to stay calm when you're around people you don't have a need to impress.

When you start to get upset, remember only one thing will put an end to it. *You* have to stop it, you must exercise self-control. You have to get hold of yourself and say, "No, I'm not getting upset." You need to remember that everywhere you go, you are a witness for the One you serve and love.

But for the Grace . . .

Though I formerly blasphemed and persecuted and
was shamefully and outrageously and aggressively
insulting [to Him], nevertheless, I obtained mercy
because I had acted out of ignorance in unbelief.

I TIMOTHY 1:13

In this Scripture Paul speaks of his past when he aggressively and vehemently persecuted Christians and had them stoned, beaten, and jailed. His ignorance was so great he actually believed God was pleased. But when Jesus appeared to him on the Damascus road, the scales fell from his eyes and he saw Truth (see Acts 9). Paul realized at that moment that he was a sinner and God's grace became a living reality in his life.

On the cross, Jesus said, "Father, forgive them, for they know not what they do" (Luke 23:34). Stephen, while being stoned, said, "Lord, fix not this sin upon them!" (Acts 7:60). What did Jesus, Paul, and Stephen have in common? They proclaimed God's grace to people who were deceived and ignorant. Recall how much mercy and grace God has given you; surely you can extend His grace to others.

The Blame Game

*And the man said, The woman whom You gave to
be with me—she gave me [fruit] from the tree, and I
ate. . . . And the woman said, The serpent beguiled
(cheated, outwitted, and deceived) me, and I ate.*

The problem has been manifesting since the beginning of time. When confronted with their sin in the Garden of Eden, Adam and Eve blamed each other, God, and the devil. This unwillingness to take personal responsibility by trying to blame anyone and anything that might be convenient, is a major cause for not living triumphantly. While in the wilderness, the Israelites complained that all of their problems were the fault of God and Moses. This was one of the major factors that kept them wandering in the wilderness for forty years, when they could have been living in the promised land.

There is nothing more emotionally painful than facing the truth about yourself and your actions. Because it is painful, most people run from it. Admitting your own mistakes and failures is difficult, but it is the only way to freedom.

Be a God Pleaser

Servants, obey in everything those who are your
earthly masters, not only when their eyes are on you
as pleasers of men, but in simplicity of purpose [with
all your heart] because of your reverence for the Lord
and as a sincere expression of your devotion to Him.

COLOSSIANS 3:22

This Scripture tells you to be a good, faithful, loyal, profitable, and hardworking employee. You are to do your job well and with a good attitude. You are not to be two-faced, showing your employer what you think he wants to see and then doing differently when he is not around. You need to be real, sincere, honest, and trustworthy.

Do you know what happens when you do your work with all your heart and soul, and do it not unto men but unto God? You receive your reward from Him, not your boss. You can look to the Lord for the reward you truly deserve. Tomorrow, decide to please God and His blessings will follow.

Enter His Rest

*And He raised us up together with Him and
made us sit down together [giving us joint
seating with Him] in the heavenly sphere
[by virtue of our being] in Christ Jesus.*

EPHESIANS 2:6

There are many places in the Bible where
Jesus, after the Resurrection, is described
as being seated. We might think standing would be
more powerful. But being seated has special signifi-
cance.

Under the Law, when a priest entered the Holy
of Holies to make sacrifices for the people's sins, he
could not sit. He had to keep moving and working
the entire time. If the bells on his robe stopped ring-
ing, that meant that he had done something wrong
and had fallen over dead.

That is why it is so awesome that Jesus ascended
into heaven and sat down as our high priest. He entered the rest of God. As joint heirs with Christ, we
can sit too. We no longer have to work and strive to
atone for our sins. Choose to rest in His presence
tonight.

A Big Dose of Humility

*For in posing as judge and passing sentence on
another, you condemn yourself, because you who judge
are habitually practicing the very same things [that
you censure and denounce].*

ROMANS 2:1

Humility is defined as "freedom from pride
and arrogance . . . a modest estimate of
one's own worth." In theology, it means having a
consciousness of your own defects. We often judge
other people because we don't really have a conscious awareness of our own flaws. We look at everybody else through a magnifying glass, but we look at
ourselves through rose-colored glasses. For others
who make mistakes, "there is no excuse," but it seems
for us, there is always a reason why our behavior is
acceptable.

The Bible says to "humble yourselves . . . under
the mighty hand of God" (1 Peter 5:6). Examine
your own heart and actions and humble yourself before Him. God gives us an opportunity to humble
ourselves, but if we refuse, He will do it for us. So
pray for God to make you aware of areas that need
attention and refuse to sit in judgment on others.

The Standby

But the Comforter (Counselor, Helper, Intercessor,
Advocate, Strengthener, Standby), the Holy Spirit,
Whom the Father will send in My name [in My
place, to represent Me and act on My behalf],
He will teach you all things.

JOHN 14:26

As the third person of the Trinity, the Holy Spirit has a personality. He can be offended and grieved and He must be treated with great respect. Once you have the understanding that He lives inside those who believe, you should do everything you can to make him feel welcome. The Holy Spirit is a Gentleman. He will not push His way into your daily affairs. If given an invitation, He is quick to respond, but He must be invited.

The Holy Spirit is always available. The *Amplified Bible* calls Him the Standby. That is a wonderful description! Think of Him ready and waiting at all times in case you need anything at all. Every single day, no matter what you may face the Holy Spirit is standing by you. Invite him to get involved in everything you do.

Finish the Journey

And Terah took Abram his son, Lot the son of
Haran, his grandson, and Sarai his daughter-in-law,
his son Abram's wife, and they went forth together to
go from Ur of the Chaldees into the land of Canaan;
but when they came to Haran, they settled there.

GENESIS 11:31

God gave Abram's father an opportunity to go to the place of His blessing—Canaan. But instead of going all the way with the Lord, he chose to stop and settle in Haran. Many believers do what Terah did. They start out for one place and settle somewhere else along the way.

It is easy to get excited when God first directs you to do something. But many times you never finish what you start because the road gets difficult. It would be nice to reap the benefits of the journey without actually having to leave your comfort zone, but it doesn't work that way. To receive your blessing, you must be willing to push on through to the finish.

Don't Look Back

Weeping may endure for a night,
but joy comes in the morning.

PSALM 30:5

Ecclesiastes 3 tells us there is a time for everything—a time to weep and a time to mourn; a time to laugh and a time to play. You'd be coldhearted and lacking compassion if you experienced loss and felt nothing. But after a while you must let go of what lies behind and press forward. If you don't, the past will destroy your future.

God said, "Moses My servant is dead. So now arise [take his place], go over this Jordan, you and all this people, into the land which I am giving to them, the Israelites. Every place upon which the sole of your foot shall tread, that have I given to you, as I promised Moses" (Joshua 1:2-3). Like the children of Israel, God wants you to let go of the past and take new ground. Don't spend the rest of your life mourning something you have lost. Go forward and don't look back.

Avoid Selective Hearing

Whatever He says to you, do it.

JOHN 2:5

An interesting truth about your ability to hear God's voice is that when you are unwilling to hear in one area of your life, it may render you unable to hear in other areas. Sometimes you turn a deaf ear to what you know the Lord is clearly saying to you—it's called "selective hearing." After a while people think they can't hear from God anymore, but in reality there are lots of things they already know He wants them to respond to and they haven't done so.

If you really want to hear from God you can't approach Him with selective hearing, hoping to narrow the topics down to only what you want to hear. Don't just go to God and talk to Him when you want or need something; also spend time just listening. He will speak to you about many issues if you will be still before Him and simply listen. Then, be sure to obey His direction.

Not Too Hard

For this commandment which I command you this
day is not too difficult for you, nor is it far off.
DEUTERONOMY 30:11

Have you ever caught yourself telling God, "I know You want me to do this, but it's just too hard!" The enemy tries to inject this phrase into your mind so you will give up. But this Scripture assures you that even when things seem impossible, nothing God expects from you is too difficult to accomplish.

The reason the Lord's commands are not too hard is because He gives you His Spirit to work in you powerfully and to help you in all He has asked. Things get hard when you are trying to do them on your own without leaning and relying on God's grace. If you know God has asked you to do something, don't back down just because it seems hard. When things get difficult, spend more time with Him, lean more on Him, and receive more grace from Him (Hebrews 4:16).

Words of Life

Death and life are in the power of the tongue,
and they who indulge in it shall eat the fruit
of it [for death or life].

PROVERBS 18:21

Think about it for a moment—death and life are in the power of the tongue. Do you have any idea what that really means? It means you and I go through life with an awesome power—not unlike fire or electricity or nuclear energy—right under our noses. It is an energy source that can produce death or life, depending on how it is used.

With this power you have the capacity for great good or great evil, for great benefit or great harm. You can use it to create death and destruction, or you can use it to create life and health. You can speak forth sickness, disease, dissention, and disaster, or you can speak forth healing, harmony, exhortation, and edification. Tonight, choose to speak life into every situation.

Love Is Selfless

Love endures long and is patient and kind; love never is envious nor boils over with jealousy, is not boastful or vainglorious, does not display itself haughtily. It is not conceited (arrogant and inflated with pride); it is not rude (unmannerly) and does not act unbecomingly. Love (God's love in us) does not insist on its own rights or its own way.

1 CORINTHIANS 13:4-5

Why do we start wars over petty things? Usually because we want to be right and we want our way, which is selfishness. The solution is love. You simply must learn to love peace and harmony, and to love them with all your being. You need to love them more than you love being right or having your own way.

This is what Paul meant when he said, "I die daily" (1 Corinthians 15:31). Dying to self is something you and I are going to have to do on a daily basis if we are to maintain peace and harmony with one another. It may hurt our flesh to adapt or adjust to someone else instead of fighting to get our own way, but in the end we will reap a life of peace and joy that is a great reward.

Peace in the House

Fill up and complete my joy by living in harmony
and being of the same mind and one in purpose,
having the same love, being in full accord and
of one harmonious mind and intention.

PHILIPPIANS 2:2

When Jesus sent the disciples out two by two to do miracles, signs, and wonders, in essence He said to them, "Go and find a house and say, 'Peace be unto you.' And if your peace settles on that house, you can stay there. If it doesn't, shake the dust off your feet and go on" (see Mark 6:7-11).

One day God showed me what Jesus was really saying to them: "I want you to go out with the anointing, but to do that you need to have peace in the house." You need to do whatever you can to maintain peace in your home because it dramatically affects the anointing and power of God that rests on your life. Keep the strife out of your life! No peace, no power! Know peace, know power!

Encourage and Edify

Let each of you esteem and look upon and be
concerned for not [merely] his own interests,
but also each for the interests of others.

PHILIPPIANS 2:4

The minute someone hurts you . . . the moment you experience disappointment—the devil begins to whisper lies about how unjustly you have been treated. All you need to do is listen to the thoughts rushing into your mind during such times and you will quickly realize how the enemy uses self-pity to keep you in bondage. However, God's Word gives you no liberty to feel sorry for yourself. Instead, we are to encourage and edify one another in the Lord.

There is a gift of compassion, which is having godly pity toward others who are hurting. But self-pity is perverted, because it is taking something God intended to be given to others and turning it in on yourself. You should live your life as 1 Thessalonians 5:11 says, "Therefore encourage (admonish, exhort) one another and edify (strengthen and build up) one another."

He Who Laughs Lasts

The kings of the earth take their places; the rulers take counsel together against the Lord and His Anointed One (the Messiah, the Christ). They say, let us break Their bands [of restraint] asunder and cast Their cords [of control] from us. He Who sits in the heavens laughs; the Lord has them in derision [and in supreme contempt He mocks them].

PSALM 2:2-4

When God's enemies gather against Him, He sits in the heavens and laughs. He is the Alpha and Omega, the Beginning and the Ending, so He already knows how things are going to turn out.

We spend too much time looking at what is taking place now instead of looking at the finish line. Like Abraham, you can laugh the laugh of faith. When God told him He would do the impossible— that even though he was too old, God would give him a child—Abraham laughed! (see Genesis 17:17) Tonight, laugh with confidence in the face of the enemy. God has already won!

Uncommon and Extraordinary

*Now to Him Who, by (in consequence of) the
[action of His] power that is at work within us, is
able to [carry out His purpose and] do super-
abundantly, far over and above all that we [dare]
ask or think [infinitely beyond our highest prayers,
desires, thoughts, hopes, or dreams].*

EPHESIANS 3:20

God uses common, ordinary people who
have uncommon goals and visions. You
should not be content to be average. Average is basically okay. It is not bad, but it is also not excellent. It
is just good enough to get by, and that isn't what
God wants for you. You don't serve an average God.
Therefore you don't have to settle for an average
life.

Every single person can be mightily used by
God. You can do great and mighty things if you believe God can use you and if you will be daring
enough to have an uncommon goal and vision.
These things won't make sense to the mind—you
have to believe God for them.

A Holy Thing

*The angel Gabriel was sent from God to a town of
Galilee named Nazareth, to a girl never having been
married and a virgin engaged to be married to a man
whose name was Joseph, a descendant of the house of
David; and the virgin's name was Mary. And he came
to her and said, Hail, O favored one [endued with
grace]! The Lord is with you! . . . And listen! You
will become pregnant and will give birth to a Son,
and you shall call His name Jesus.*

LUKE 1:26-28,31

When Gabriel appeared to Mary, the
Holy Spirit came upon her and planted in
her womb a "Holy Thing." This Seed was the Son of
God sent to deliver mankind from sin.

When you are born again, a "Holy Thing," the
Holy Spirit, is planted in you. As you water that
Seed with God's Word, it will grow into a giant tree
of righteousness, "the planting of the Lord, that He
may be glorified" (Isaiah 61:3).

Roll Away the Reproach

And the Lord said to Joshua, This day have I rolled
away the reproach of Egypt from you. So the name of
the place is called Gilgal [rolling] to this day.

JOSHUA 5:9

The Lord ordered that all the Israelite males be circumcised, since this had not been done during the entire forty years they had wandered in the Wilderness. After this was done, the Lord told Joshua He had "rolled away" the reproach (blame, disgrace, and shame) of Egypt from His people. When God said this, He was making a point. Egypt represents the world. After a few years of being in the world, we all need the reproach of it rolled away.

For God to roll away the reproach from you means you must receive for yourself the forgiveness He is offering for all your past sins. It is impossible to deserve God's blessings—you can only humbly accept and appreciate them, and be in awe of how good He is and how much He loves you.

Minding Our Own Business

*When Peter saw him [John], he said to Jesus, Lord,
what about this man? Jesus said to him, If I want him
to stay (survive, live) until I come, what is that to
you? [What concern is it of yours?] You follow Me!*

JOHN 21:21,22

Jesus was talking with Peter about the
hardships he would have to endure in order to serve and glorify Him. As soon as Jesus finished speaking, Peter turned, spotted John and
immediately asked Jesus what His will was for him.
Peter wanted to make sure that if he was going to go
through rough times, so would John. Jesus politely
told Peter to mind his own business.

You should be encouraged and take hope in the
fact that Jesus' disciples struggled with many of the
same things you do. Jealousy, envy, and comparing
yourself with others is childish. As with the disciples, Jesus has great patience with you. But it helps
to remember that minding our own business is more
than enough for us to handle.

Learn to Enjoy Him

But You are a God ready to pardon, gracious and
merciful, slow to anger, and of great steadfast love.

NEHEMIAH 9:17

The highest call on your life is to enjoy God. But you can't enjoy Him if you are convinced He is upset with you. Jesus came to deliver you from the wrong kind of fear in your relationship with your heavenly Father. You should be relaxed in His presence. You need to have reverential fear—the kind that provokes respect, honor, and obedience. But you must refuse to believe any thoughts that the Lord is angry with you.

You are no surprise to God. Jeremiah 1:5 states that before He formed you in the womb, God knew you! He knew what He was getting when He drew you into relationship with Himself. He already knows the things you will do wrong in the future. God is not nearly as hard to get along with as you think He is. It is not your sin that hinders you—it is unbelief!

Dwell in Unity

Behold, how good and how pleasant it is for
brethren to dwell together in unity!

PSALM 133:1

Great power was manifested in the lives of the early believers. Acts 2:46 tells us why: "And day after day they regularly assembled in the temple with united purpose." They had the same vision, the same goal, and they were all pressing toward the same mark. They prayed in agreement (see Acts 4:24), lived in harmony (see Acts 2:44), cared for one another (see Acts 2:46), met each other's needs (see Acts 4:34), and lived a life of faith (see Acts 4:31). The early church lived in unity—and operated in great power.

Now the church is divided into countless factions with different opinions about everything. Even individual congregations are split by the most trivial differences. When we finally see Jesus face-to-face, we will surely discover that not one of us was 100 percent right. Only love holds people together. Make a strong commitment to do whatever is necessary to live in unity—you will discover how good it is!

He Is Strong

We are weak, but you are [so very] strong!
1 CORINTHIANS 4:10

We need help—and a lot of it. Jeremiah 10:23 says, "the way of a man is not in himself; it is not in man [even in a strong man or in a man at his best] to direct his [own] steps." It really is impossible for man to properly run his own life. Admitting that fact is not a sign of weakness, it is a sign of spiritual maturity. You are weak unless you find your strength in God, and the sooner you face that fact, the better.

Many people have position, wealth, and power, but they may not have what really matters—good relationships, right standing with God, peace, joy, contentment, satisfaction, good health, and the ability to enjoy life. Not everything that appears well is well! You may be trying hard to make things work out right and always failing. Your problem is not that you are a failure. Your problem is simply that you have not gone to the right source for help.

A New Thing

Behold, I am doing a new thing! Now it
springs forth; do you not perceive and know it
and will you not give heed to it?

ISAIAH 43:19

Do you ever get really tired of doing the same old thing all the time? You want to do something different but you either don't know what to do, or you are afraid to do the new thing you are thinking about doing?

You often get into ruts. You do the same thing all the time even though you are bored with it because you are afraid to step out and do something different. You would rather be safe and bored than excited and living on the edge. There is a certain amount of comfort in sameness—you may not like it, but you are familiar with it.

God has created you to need and crave diversity and variety. You require freshness and newness in your life. As this year and this day come to an end, make a quality decision to step out into the new thing God has for you. And don't forget to enjoy yourself!

About the Author

JOYCE MEYER has been teaching the Word of God since 1976 and in full-time ministry since 1980. She is the bestselling author of more than sixty inspirational books, including *In Pursuit of Peace*, *How to Hear from God*, *Knowing God Intimately*, and *Battlefield of the Mind*. She has also released thousands of teaching cassettes and a complete video library. Joyce's *Enjoying Everyday Life* radio and television programs are broadcast around the world, and she travels extensively conducting conferences. Joyce and her husband, Dave, are the parents of four grown children and make their home in St. Louis, Missouri.

To Contact the Author Write:

Joyce Meyer Ministries
P O. Box 655
Fenton, Missouri 63026
or call: (636) 349-0303
Internet Address: www.joycemeyer.org

Your prayer requests are welcome.

To contact the author
in Canada, please write:
Joyce Meyer Ministries Canada, Inc.
Lambeth Box 1300
London, ON N6P IT5
or call: (636) 349-0303

In Australia, please write:
Joyce Meyer Ministries-Australia
Locked Bag 77

Queensland 4122
or call: 07 3349 1200

In England, please write:
Joyce Meyer Ministries
PO Box 1549
Windsor
SL4 1 GT
or call: (o) 1753-831102

In South Africa, please write:
Joyce Meyer Ministries
PO Box 5
SOUTH AFRICA
(27) 21-701-1056

Books by Joyce Meyer

Battlefield of the Mind

Battlefield of the Mind Study Guide

Approval Addiction

Ending Your Day Right

In Pursuit of Peace

The Secret Power of Speaking God's Word

Seven Things That Steal Your Joy

Starting Your Day Right

Beauty for Ashes Revised Edition

How to Hear from God

How to Hear from God Study Guide

Knowing God Intimately

The Power of Forgiveness

The Power of Determination

The Power of Being Positive

The Secrets of Spiritual Power

The Battle Belongs to the Lord

Secrets to Exceptional Living

Eight Ways to Keep the Devil Under Your Feet

Teenagers Are People Too!

Filled with the Spirit

Celebration of Simplicity

The Joy of Believing Prayer

Never Lose Heart

Healing the Brokenhearted

Me and My Big Mouth!

Me and My Big Mouth! Study Guide

Prepare to Prosper

Do It Afraid!

Expect a Move of God in Your Life . . . Suddenly!

Enjoying Where You Are on the Way to Where You Are Going

The Most Important Decision You Will Ever Make

When, God, When?

Why, God, Why?

The Word, the Name, the Blood

Tell Them I Love Them

Peace

The Root of Rejection

If Not for the Grace of God

If Not for the Grace of God Study Guide

JOYCE MEYER SPANISH TITLES

*Las Siete Cosas Que Te Roban el Gozo (Seven Things That
Steal Your Joy)*

Empezando Tu Día Bien (Starting Your Day Right)

BY DAVE MEYER

Life Lines

Notes

Nevin

Emma & Eden   healthy & safe

Great health

Good friends

employment

place to rest

food provision

Supportive parents

loving siblings

Great in laws

Eden born healthy

Entire family recovered H1N1

Awesome summer camp Good moved

Notes